APPLY THE LAWS IN THIS
SERIES AND EXPERIENCE

TRANSFIGURATION

Sister Thedra

Volume V

Copyright © 2021 by Halls of Light, LLC

All rights reserved. This book or any portion thereof may not be reproduced or used in any manner whatsoever without the express written permission of the publisher except for the use of brief quotations in a book review.

ISBN: 978-1-7373071-5-0

TRANSFIGURATION

A complete change of form or appearance into a more beautiful or spiritual state. "in this light the junk undergoes a transfiguration; it shines"

The transfiguration is a sign that Jesus was to fulfill the Law and the prophets. It also assured James, Peter, and John the Jesus was indeed the Messiah.

In Christian teachings, the Transfiguration is a pivotal moment, and the setting on the mountain is presented as the point where human nature meets God: the meeting place for the temporal and the eternal, with Jesus himself as the connecting point, acting as the bridge between heaven and earth.

To the Reader

Please read and review "Divine Explanations"
on page 237 for questions and definitions of terms.

This book is only a portion of the teachings and prophecies that have been given by Sananda (Jesus Christ), Sanat Kumara, and others of the higher realms, and Recorded by Sister Thedra.

Dedications

These volumes, entitled TRANSFIGURATION are dedicated to Sheryl McCartney and Kamalakar Durgapu, without whose invaluable assistance this work would not have been possible.

Contents

BE YE NOT BOUND BY OPINIONS 1

THE GATE IS GUARDED WELL 43

THE KING OF GLORY COMETH 93

ARISE UNTO THY STATION 149

SEAL OF SOLOMON 195

Mission Statement 230

Sananda's Appearance 231

About the Late Sister Thedra 232

Divine Explanations 237

Other Books by TNT Publishing 248

Esu Jesus Sananda

This reproduction is from an actual photograph taken on June 1st, 1961, in Chichen Itza, Yucatan, by one of thirty archaeologists working in the area at the time. Sananda appeared in visible, tangible body and permitted His photograph to be taken.

BE YE NOT BOUND BY OPINIONS

Bor speaking:-

Sori Sori Sori

Praise unto the Father God -- Praise the name of Solen forever and forever -- Praise the Father-Mother God forevermore ---

By their GRACE and their MERCY shall ye be brot out of bondage and for this have ye waited -- By thy own effort shall ye prepare thyself that ye may be delivered out ---

Wherein is it written: "None takes thee out - against thy will".

Be ye of a mind to return unto thy abiding place - and ye shall be delivered out forever and forever -- So be it and be it so -- Amen and Selah

By thy own efforts shall ye be delivered - I say ye and ye alone are the ones which hold thyself bound - for nothing can hold thee against thy will ---

Because ye have followed the dragon - and because ye are of a mind to serve him are ye held in bondage -- Ye have served him with all thy might - all thy time -- All thy strength have ye devoted unto him ---

Little time have ye given unto thy own deliverance - for ye separate thyself from the source of thy being - ye go in and out the dragon's den with little thot of thy God - thy divinity -- Ye forget that ye have been offered thy freedom - ye forget what has been said unto thee from the realms of Light ---

Ye forget not that which <u>they</u> say unto thee - ye fret and cry over that which <u>they</u> say - and ye turn thy face from the Source ---

Ye call out for help from <u>them</u> and they hear thee - yet they do not deliver thee out - for they are yet in darkness - they are as thou art - bound within the dragon's den - they serve him and know it not ---

Now will ye not seek thy Source of being and return unto it? Be not bound by opinions and the puny will of man - for it is as a millstone upon thy back -- Ye shall free thyself of all thy opinions and of thy own legirons ---

Be ye of a <u>mind</u> to learn - lay aside thy old preconceived ideas - use thy own free will that ye may be unbound - and let no man say which way ye shall go ---

Forgive them which would bind thee - and give unto them NO power to hold thee – I say ye battle against them - yet ye need NOT - for thy own will to be unbound shall be thy Shield and thy Buckler ---

Be ye as one which has the mind to comprehend that which I say unto thee ---

Go thy way in PEACE and thanksgiving and bless this day - for it is now come when ye shall come to know many things which ye have not known since ye went into darkness - Ye are fortuned to be within the Earth at this time for a great and divine plan -- I am with thee unto the end ---

I am thy older brother and thy Sibor - Bor

Sister Thedra of the Emerald Cross

The Living Sacrifice

Sarah speaking: -

While ye are yet bound within the earthly vehicle - ye shall be as one which has thy hand in mine - and I shall lead thee from out thy bondage -- I shall give unto thee as ye are prepared to receive ---

I shall give unto thee as a Mother gives unto the child - and I shall be as thy Mother Eternal - I shall not deceive thee nor shall I deny thee.

I shall bestow upon thee my love and all that I have - I shall bless thee with my being - I shall hold thee fast in the hours of thy trial - I shall bless thee with my very being ---

I shall speak unto thee in the hours of thy sleep - I shall cause thee to remember that which I have said - I shall await thy return unto me and I shall be glad for thy return ---

Bring unto the altar thy heart - thy hands as a living sacrifice - that ye may purchase thy own passport into the place wherein I am - for nought else shall redeem thyself ---

When it is come that ye surrender up thyself - a host of light workers shall come unto thee for the purpose of assisting thee in thy flight -- Such is their part - yet ye shall do thy part - that is of preparing thyself for to receive them - so be it thy part ---

I say unto thee: Be ye true unto thyself and turn thy face homeward for it is now come when great shall be thy work which shall be given unto thee to do - and great shall be thy responsibility - for many shall turn unto thee and ask of thee the way -- I say many shall come unto thee to ask of thee the way - and they shall be heard and answered -- So be it and Selah

I am come that they may be answered -- So be it and Selah

I am thy Mother Sarah - Mother of Abraham

Sister Thedra of the Emerald Cross

Ye May Betray Thyself - NOT the Hiarchi

Sananda speaking:-

Blest art thou O my children - I come unto thee as thou hast come that there might be light within the world of man - I say that there might be light in the world of man---

For it is now come when they have forgotten their Source of being and they are not of a mind to see the light within the Father's realm ---

They run to and fro and seek within dark places for wisdom - wherein is no wisdom - and the law prevents them from that which they strive to attain ---

I say they shall find no wisdom - no peace - until they turn unto the Source of their being -- Blest are they which do turn unto Him - God the Father ---

That which was given unto them in ages past that they may comprehend such laws as govern the Earth and the elements have been misused - <u>mis</u>-interpreted - and they have been adulterated and they have been given unto the unjust and imprudent -- They have added to and taken from them - until now - there is little Left which would be unto thee or any value ---

I say ye have not had the records revealed unto thee - ye have been as ones running hither and yon - seeking wisdom -- Ye have not sought thy freedom in the realms of light ---

Ye are blinded by thy own simple foolishness - ye are in the thinkers realm - ye are as ones <u>unenlightened</u> - ye know not - for the law governing the elements shall be held in trust for the day when they are prepared to use it for the good of all mankind ---

I say ye shall not conquest the planets of thy solar system ---

Ye shall not pilfer the plans which has been held for the initiate ---

Ye shall not betray the Hiarchi -- Ye may betray thyself - NOT the Hiarchi ---

The Father has given unto the children of Earth the new dispensation which is designed to free thee - yet ye make laws to bind them - ye make weapons which are designed to destroy them -- Ye are as judge which sit in high places - ye are as the parrots - ye parrot thy sayings - thy opinions -- Ye are as bigots - ye are hypocrites - ye sell and barter the tools of Satan - ye are of the mind to serve him - ye are not of a mind to turn from him - ye go into the dragon's den with thy hand out -- Ye go into the places set aside as the temple of the Living God - ye wear thy mask - ye wear thy gaudy clothing -- Ye care not for thy poor - ye care not for the suffering ---

I say thy penny is of no value - ye cannot buy thy way into the Kingdom of God ---

Ye give thy penny of no value - while ye withhold thy love and thyself -- I say again: Give unto God the Father - thy heart - thy hand - thy will ---

Many go into the places wherein they lie dying - they fear to touch them - they shudder at the stench -- They refrain from going because they cannot bear the sight of them which are sick - blind - lame and deaf - them which are their brothers - they fear for themself ---

Why - O why are ye so blind - why are ye so doleful?

Ye indulge thyself - ye give not of thyself ---

When - O children will ye awaken? I stand with hands tied - I cry unto thee in the name of our Father which has sent me unto thee: AWAKEN - AWAKEN! I am come that ye might awaken ---

I say unto ye sleeper: Many are ascending unto the Father this day as ones freed from all bondage forever - free - forever free - and ye know it not - ye sleep on ---

O Father - I have come into the Earth at thy will - why do they not know me? O Father - cause them to awaken! Thy will be done for them thru me - thy Son - Amen -- So be it and be it so ---

I am Sananda

Hallelujah -- Amen -- Praise His Holy Name

Sister Thedra of the Emerald Cross

Bor's Ascension
Temple of Panamanche - Island of Terrawatta

Sori Sori

Bor speaking:-

Blest be ye this day - blest am I that I am prepared to come unto thee thusly - for I am of the Father sent that ye may have light ---

Poor in spirit are they which do not receive of the light - for they cut themself off without the substance of life ---

Poor in spirit are they which turn from their Source -- Poor in spirit are they which think themself wise - they shall be found without substance ---

I am sent of God the Father that ye may have light -- I come unto thee as one qualified of Him - the Father - that I might give unto thee a guiding hand -- I have worked in silence lo the many centuries - from the time of my initiation within the land of the Andes - wherein I was prepared for my ascension by many of the great initiates - our beloved Brother Maheru being the Grand Master within the Temple of Panamanche - wherein many ascended even as I - Now I shall relate for them which are fortuned to read these words - my own ascension - which was from the beginning part of this plan ---

When I was a young man of mature age I lived on the west shore of Africa wherein flourished a great and grand civilization which has been lost in antiquity -- Ye have no knowledge of its beauty and science - for from it grew many branches which are likewise lost to mankind ---

When it came that I was prepared for this part of my preparation for the "Greater Part"- I was brot thru the interior of the Earth - called the "Inner Way"- and we entered that great and glorious Temple of Panamanche of the island of Terrawatta of the Andes Mountains ---

Now ye - my Sister Thedra - shall remember my account given on that place wherein ye recorded the first account which was given unto thee ---

Ye were within that place called Terrawatta with me at the time of my ascension - ye saw that part of my preparation -- This account is part of that which was given unto thee to be done at this time -- Ye accepted this part - and it is as yet not finished - for it is near time when again we shall come together face to face - and ye shall remember me and it shall seem as a day since that great day when we stood upon the great golden altar and received the blessings of our beloved and blessed Brother Sanat Kumara - which was even then the Comanche -- Be ye blest of him as I have been blest ---

I shall bring unto thee one which shall speak with thee at a later hour -- I am prepared to speak at that time ---

I am Bor

Sister Thedra of the Emerald Cross

Forget Not Thy Benefactors

Bor speaking:-

Blessings from the throne of the Most High Living God -- Be ye blest of me and of my presence ---

I come unto thee as one prepared for to give thee as I have received of the Father-Mother God ---

I declare for thee that which the Father has willed unto thee -- I declare for thee that which is thy rightful inheritance ---

I declare for thee that which is thine by direct inheritance -- I say ye are the children of God the Father - and none shall deny thee thy inheritance - which is willed unto thee ---

Ye shall now declare for thyself that which is thy own by divine right and direct inheritance -- Ye shall be as ones prepared to receive that which has been kept for thee for this day ---

Ye have forfeited thy inheritance - yet ye shall now claim it - and ye shall be as ones prepared to receive it and ye shall be glad ---

For it is now come when ye shall come to know thy own power - and thy own power which has been held concealed within thy own flame shall be revealed unto thee ---

Ye shall have the power revealed unto thee when ye have proven thyself worthy of such power -- And none shall put within thy hand the rod and the staff - before ye are prepared to use it with love - wisdom and justice ---

I say as ye are prepared - so shall ye receive - be ye as ones prepared for the greater part ---

Now ye shall come to know that which is meant by the <u>greater part</u> for ye which are prepared shall be participants in the great and grand plan - which is brot forth thru the Hiarchi -- And when ye have prepared thyself to receive such revelations - ye shall be brot into the secret place wherein we which sit in council for thy benefit do dwell - and wherein we do keep vigil for thy safety - and wherein ye shall sit in council for the benefit of all mankind - and wherein ye shall have the laws expounded and revealed - and ye shall see the wisdom of thy preparation - and ye shall rejoice that this day is come ---

Praise His Holy Name - Solen Solen - Aum Solen ---

Be ye as one which has my hand upon thee and I shall bless thee - and I shall stand ready to assist thee -- Call and I shall answer thee - for I do hear thee and I come at thy call ---

I say - forget not the cause of thy being - and forget not thy Benefactors which are sent to assist thee -- I am thy servant in the name of the Most High Living God -- Amen and Selah ---

I am Bor

Sister Thedra of the Emerald Cross

I am Eternally a Virgin - ...Nameless - Formless - Soundless

Blest are they which come unto this altar in the name of the Father - Son and Holy Ghost -- Amen -- So be it ---

I come that ye may have light - I come that ye may be brot out of bondage - I come that ye may return unto thy abiding place - I am come that ye may know as I know - I am come that ye may be even as I AM and I am ONE with the Father-Mother God ---

I AM - and I know myself to be - I have not separated myself from them - I am one with them - and I am for that part - not of a mind to separate myself from them -- I go not out from them - neither do I take upon myself a body of flesh substance -- I am eternally a virgin - I create not - neither am I created -- I AM - have been and always shall be - I was before Abraham was - and I shall be when all the galaxies shall pass from their spheres ---

I AM - and I am nameless - I am formless - I am soundless - yet I am all these things -- Without me there would be no-thing - I AM that I AM - ye name it and that I AM ---

I come not - neither do I go - I am ever present -- I am the beginning and the end - yet I have no beginning and I have no end -- I am neither male or female - I am neither black or white ---

I am not confined to any sphere - neither am I confined unto any octave - any part of any system -- No galaxy - no place contains me - no part binds me - I am freedom - I am boundless --

I am neither great nor small - I am all that which is REAL -- I AM I AM and ever shall be ---

I AM because I AM - and none shall limit me by naming me - yet I am called by many names -- No man knows me - for I am the unknown the unknown which is UN-knowable - I am the Alpha and Omega -- I go within - I go without - I am within - I am without - yet I go not - neither do I come - I AM ---

I give not - neither do I take - I need not for I am all things - I AM and for this thou art ---

Awaken! Awaken and be ye as one come alive! ye deaf and blind - Hear ye and see ye - and ye shall be brot out of bondage -- So be it and Selah ---

I AM

Sister Thedra of the Emerald Cross

Our Source of Being

Sarah speaking: -

Beloved children: I come unto thee for the purpose of bringing the home -- I am thy Mother eternal - and I am the fortune of thy MALE PARENT GOD -- Ye are because we are - ye have been given form and being because we are - ye are because we are - because we called thee forth ---

Ye are now called out from darkness - from all thy bondages and we offer unto thee thy freedom from all bondage - as thy inheritance willed unto thee from the beginning -- Blest are they which receive it this day ---

I now speak unto my children as I have not spoken from the beginning - for it is now finished - when ye shall now be done with the dark path which ye have chosen -- Ye shall go out from me no more - ye shall walk with me and talk with me - ye shall know thyself - and forget not that ye are ONE with me ---

And ye shall have no need for the trapping of darkness - ye shall have no need for all that which has bound thee within the dragon's den I say ye are bound within the dragon's den - and ye know not by what ye are bound -- Blest are they which are unbound ---

I say unto thee my children: When ye are of a mind to learn - when ye are so willed to accept thy inheritance in full - ye shall have a host of light workers rush to thy side which shall give unto thee a hand - and ye shall not want - neither shall ye weary in well doing ---

Blest are they which do turn unto me - for I shall give unto them that which is theirs by divine right -- I am with thee and I shall bless thee as I have waited to bless thee ---

I say my children: I have waited long for this day when ye should turn thy face homeward - and when ye might receive that which was willed unto thee in the beginning -- Be ye as ones which can accept it.

By the Grace of thy Father-Mother shall ye return ---

Be ye at Peace and Poise and I shall abide with thee ---

I am thy Eternal Mother Sarah

Posite-Posa shall speak unto thee later --

Sister Thedra of the Emerald Cross

Be Ye a Living Example of the Initiate

Sananda speaking: -

My beloved children: I come unto thee as one of the Father sent - I come that ye may be blest as I have been blest - I give unto thee my hand - I give unto thee of myself that ye may know as I know - I come that where I go ye may go also ---

Be ye blest of me and by me - and give unto me thy hand - and I shall lead thee into the place wherein ye shall stand before the Great White Altar and receive thy freedom - wherein ye shall stand face to face with me ---

I come that ye may awaken from thy dream state - and that ye may come alive and that ye may be forever free ---

I say - many know not that I am within the Earth - yet ye know me and ye have walked with me and talked with me and ye know that I AM ---

Now ye shall give unto them this word - and they shall bear witness of these my words unto thee - and no man shall call me a liar - for I say that which the Father would have me say - and I bear witness of Him - and none shall cut me off or close the door against me ---

I say - woe unto them which bear false witness against me or my prophets -- Now when it is come that they bear false witness against me or my prophets - the law shall be set against them and it shall deal justly and promptly ---

I say it is no respecter of persons - and it is the law that anyone which-so-ever does place themself greater than the law is forced to face his own folly -- Par for par shall he be meted out his due - I say he shall be unto himself judge - and he shall be brot face to face with his own self - he shall be brot to justice -- I have said: A lesson learned is a lesson earned -- So be it and Selah ---

Bring thy heart and thy hand unto this altar - give of thyself that others might have light -- Be ye a living example of the initiate - and let thy light so shine that they see it and follow it -- Blest shall ye be ---

I am thy Brother and thy Sibor - Sananda - Son of God

Sister Thedra of the Emerald Cross

Transmutation

Sanat Kumara speaking on the subject of transmutation:-

Ye have recorded that which I have said - and it is clearly written while not clearly understood - nor shall it be by them which have not the mind of comprehension ---

I say it shall be revealed unto the initiate - for this is a great part of the work of the initiate which chooses to go the Royal Road -- And for this shall they which are yet in darkness wait - they shall prepare themself for such revelation ---

I say - all is according to law - and such laws shall not be subject to the poor in spirit - for they know not the responsibility of such knowledge ---

I say they are un-responsible and they are not trust worthy - sad that they be - yet that shall come forth in due time---

Ye shall be as ones mindful of thy responsibility and of the power which is given unto thee - such is thy preparation - and sad is he which betrays himself or his trust -- Blest is he which goes the Royal Road.

Speak of this not lightly - for ye have as yet not comprehended that which is spoken of herein ---

Be ye as one prepared for the greater revelation ---

I am Sanat Kumara

Sister Thedra of the Emerald Cross

Alpha & Omega

Solen speaking:-

Beloved children: I have given unto thee being - I am thy Father-Mother God -- I am not conditioned by matter - nor am I made -- I am not of the Earth - nor am I of any part of thy own Solar System - I am not of the substance of earth - I take not a flesh body - yet I cause flesh to become manifested in all planets within thy Solar System ---

I <u>cause</u> it to be made manifest - I speak and it is done -- I am not dependent upon matter - I AM matter -- I am Spirit - I am Alpha - Omega - I am all these things from which matter come ---

I am thy Father-Mother God - from which ye went out - I am thyself Born of flesh art thou - born once of me - many times of woman -- I say ye have been born once of me - many times of woman ---

Ye have passed thru the womb of woman many times in which ye have lost thy memory of me -- Ye have forgotten thy Source - ye have not remembered it - ye have had it blanked from thee when ye chose the way of Lucifer - Ye gave thy consent that it be blanked from thee - ye have forgotten even this ---

My children ye have forfeited a great inheritance - ye shall now claim it - it is thine by divine inheritance ---

Ye shall not be given anything until ye are prepared to receive it -- Ye shall now ponder these my words - and give unto thyself credit for being my Sons-daughters - and ye shall step forth in all thy radiance and claim thy Sonship which is thine -- I say ye shall step forth and claim thy inheritance I have willed unto thee from the beginning -- And ye shall be born again of me - ye shall step forth as one glorified of me and by me - for ye shall not die - ye shall not taste of death -- Ye shall be given a new body of light substance - ye shall transmute all that which ye have misused within the realms of darkness - ye shall be even as a God within thy own right - for I have willed it so ---

Ye shall be one with me and ye shall be as one qualified to give unto <u>them</u> that which ye have received - for I say - as ye receive so shall ye give unto them which follow thee ---

I say unto thee my children: Many shall come unto thee which are athirst and weary of their way - I say ye shall give unto them that which is given unto thee for them -- So be it and Selah -- I am revealed unto thee that ye may come home unto thy abiding place ---

I am thy Father Solen Aum Solen

Sister Thedra of the Emerald Cross

Beau Beauty

Sarah speaking:-

Sori Sori -- Praise His name - praise the name of Solen Aum Solen all ye children of Earth -- Praise Him - ye which have thy being in Him and in Him ye shall live and forever shall ye be with Him -- Praise Him all ye hosts which are within the realms of light - for ye shall rejoice with all thy being ---

For it is now come when great shall be the light shed in the dark places wherein they are bound - and they shall be unbound and they shall be freed from all bondage - and they shall be caught up with Him and they shall be crowned with the Crown of the Sun - and they shall have upon their head the Seal of Solomon - and upon their countenance they shall wear a fortune of the Sarah Mother of God - they shall be blest of Her the Mother God - and they shall be as ones within their own right Sons of God - for they shall return unto Him as ones born of Him - born of woman no more ---

For it is now come when they which are prepared shall be glad and they shall rejoice thruout all eternity for this day ---

Praise Him -- Praise Him all ye initiates - praise Him all ye Sons of God -- Be ye lifted up - be ye as ones filled with joy and ye shall remember this day forever ---

I am with thee and I shall give unto thee as I have received -- Beau Beauty am I - and would ye not know me as Beautiful within the realm of light -- I am within the place wherein I am prepared to give unto thee as I have received - and I am the fortune of my Father -- Bountiful are His gifts - generous is He - and He has not cut thee off from him -- I say unto thee O ye of Earth: Turn thy face homeward - make thy face to shine with the joy of His Love ---

Be ye not cast down - lift up thy eyes - be ye glad of heart and give thanks in all things - blest shall ye be ---

I AM and I know myself to be one with all that is - all that shall ever be ---

I AM - I AM - I AM and ever shall be -- I am called Blessed - I am called the Mother of Abraham - I am the Mother of Abraham - I am thy Mother Eternal --

I am

Sister Thedra of the Emerald Cross

The Pure Gold ONCH

Mother Sarah speaking:-

Sori Sori Sori

Be ye blest of me - of my presence and I shall reveal unto thee many things - I shall put within thy hand the rod which shall be made of brass I shall give unto thee thy orb and the scepter ---

I shall be unto thee all which ye shall have need of - I shall give unto thee great comprehension - I shall bring thee out of bondage and bring thee into the Light of the Christ - the light which never fails -- I shall do for thee that which ye have not done - I shall be with thee at the Great White Altar when ye receive thy freedom ---

I shall give unto thee the robe which shall be white - and which shall have upon it many jewels -- I shall place about thy neck the ONCH which shall be pure gold -- I shall place within thy hand a scroll which shall have upon it written thy name which shall be new unto thee - for ye shall bear that name from that day forward -- Ye shall be as a new man - as a sister of light - as one which has received thy inheritance.

Ye shall minister unto them in the name of the Father - Son and Holy Ghost - and they shall be healed and they shall know wherein they are healed - they shall be as ones come alive and they shall come seeking their freedom -- They shall call for light - they shall turn from their way of darkness - they shall be freed from all manner of disease - they shall be as ones liberated ---

They shall be as ones which have prepared themself to receive - and for this shall they receive - blest shall they be ---

I am with thee that ye may be prepared to bless them even as I shall bless thee -- I come that ye may be unto them my hand and my foot made manifest ---

I AM and I shall BE -- When the Earth shall be no more - I shall BE -- I AM - I AM - I AM ---

I am thy Mother Eternal -

I am Sarah

Sister Thedra of the Emerald Cross

Blest are They Which Speak with God the Father

Bor speaking: -

Beloved of my being: Ye shall be as one which has my hand upon thee - and ye shall be led into the place wherein I am ---

I say we are within the place wherein we are in council for the good of all mankind - not for the good of a few - but for the good of <u>all</u> mankind - wherein there are many which await thy coming -- Ye are as one which has waited and thy waiting shall end -- So be it and Selah.

Be ye as one which has gone the long way - and I say ye shall be as one which has gone this way for the last time -- Ye shall not be at the end of the coronation - ye shall be at the ALTAR - ye shall sit at the right hand of Him which shall give unto thee thy new part - and ye shall be blest of Him and by Him and ye shall be glad -- So be it and Selah.

Be ye as one prepared - for one shall come unto thee and he shall give unto thee that for which ye have waited - blest shall ye be - blest shall they be which come unto this altar ---

Blest are they which speak with God the Father - blest shall they be Be ye blest of me and of my presence -

I am thy Brother Bor

Sister Thedra of the Emerald Cross

Ye are on the Verge of Great Discoveries

Sarnica speaking: -

Son of God am I -- I come unto thee that ye may have light-- I bring unto thee one from out the Inner Temple wherein the Father abides - wherein there is only LOVE - WISDOM and TRUTH - wherein all things are known ---

I say unto thee - ye are on the verge of great discoveries-- Blest are they which come into the place wherein all things are known - blest are they which do seek the light - blest are they which are brot out of bondage ---

Be ye blest of me and of the one which I bring - for he has not yet spoken unto them - he has spoken unto thee when ye were in the High Andes - and great was thy love for him -- Receive him now and be ye as his hand made manifest unto them - for he has much to give -- I say he shall give unto them which do receive him MUCH -- He has received his Sonship and his inheritance in full - he has returned unto his abiding place ---

Blest be ye of my presence - for I come unto thee from out the Father's realm that they may be blest of me thru thee - and so shall they be blest ---

Ye shall now say unto them as I would say - and in my name - that when they have given unto themself credit for being a Son of God - and walk in the way set before them - they shall be as ones given the necessary help - they shall be brot into the place which is prepared for them - wherein they shall be prepared for a new part which shall be given unto them to do -- They shall be as ones responsible for all that which they do and say - they shall be responsible for every thought -- Every turn of their hand shall be weighed in the balance - for all the energy with which ye work is of God the Father - and it is either used for to glorify Him or to torment thee -- I say ye either bless thyself or torment thyself with the energy which is portioned out unto thee ---

Ye have free will to choose that which ye do - yet ye are as ones responsible for that action which sets the law into motion ---

I am now prepared to step forth and to aid thee in thy search - yet in this new dispensation it has been made easier and safer for the initiate for it is now come when many shall walk among thee for the purpose of giving unto thee assistance - They shall give unto thee nought before ye have prepared thyself for to receive it - they shall withhold all their priceless pearls with wisdom until ye have reached the age of maturity and understanding and are found trustworthy - blest are they which are found trustworthy blest indeed are they ---

While ye are found wanting ye are as ones blind - ye are deaf - yet when ye are found trustworthy of all the treasure - house of knowledge ye shall be as one touched - ye shall be quickened - and ye shall be as one come alive - and ye shall know and know that ye know ---

Ye shall be sibored in the hours of thy sleep - and when ye have been so prepared ye shall be given a portion - and ye shall step from thy old body of earthly substance - into thy lighter body and ye shall go out into the ether and ye shall see the wonder of the Father's handiwork ye shall cry for joy of it - ye shall bless them which have aided thee in thy search - ye shall bless thy Benefactors - ye shall give thanks for being part of this plan - ye shall rejoice with thy Benefactors - ye shall be as one prepared for the greater part ---

Then and only then shall ye be free from all bondage - shall ye drink of the Crystal Goblet of the substance of Life - the liquid Light which shall be brot from out the heart of God the Father - and placed within the hand of one of His Sons which has likewise drunken from the Goblet ---

Beloved which do read this portion: Hear ye me - I say ye shall not be misled -- I have said many times unto this my recorder - that one shall come unto thee which shall hold within his hand a Crystal Goblet beautiful beyond description - and he shall offer it unto thee - I say ye shall ask to drink -- I say unto thee my beloved children: Drink deeply and ye shall not die -- Praise His name - Solen Aum Solen ---

Son of God am I -- Be ye blest this day

Sister Thedra of the Emerald Cross

The Subject of Waiting

Sananda speaking: -

Beloved of my being: One which has come unto this altar - alone have ye come - yet I say ye are not alone for I am with thee -- I am near unto thee - I shall not forsake thee for I have given unto thee this part - I have prepared thee - I have given unto thee of myself that ye may be prepared for thy new part ---

I say ye shall walk among them as one made new - as one made whole - as one glorified of God the Father -- So be it and Selah -- I am one with the Father which has sent me - and I say ye are as one which shall be brot out from the place wherein ye are as one prepared for the greater part -- So be it and Selah---

Now will it not be for the good of all mankind that ye be brot into the place wherein I am - and I say ye shall bring one with thee which is yet within the world of men -- He has gone out from the place wherein ye are and he has gone within his own place of another which he has chosen for himself - and he has chosen for himself that which he shall do - and he has but to be reminded of his benefactors - and he shall be reminded and he shall have his memory restored unto him and he shall be as one come alive - and he shall be as one reminded of his Source of being - and he shall be glad for his remembering -- So be it and Selah.

Now say unto them which have come in - that they shall have upon themselves the responsibility of their own preparation - and for this have they been given the law governing their preparation -- For it is now come when they which are to come shall walk among thee to seek out the ones which are prepared - and I say - sad shall they be which is found wanting ---

I am now going to speak unto thee on the subject of waiting: - Be ye as ones prepared for this day - and ye shall be glad - for ye which do wait shall be found wanting - ye shall be caught up short of thy course I say - wait and ye shall be found wanting - and ye shall be caught up short of thy course -- Poor in spirit is he which waits ---

Now ye shall give much thought unto these my words - ponder them long and ask that ye may be as one prepared -- And yet I say - ye shall do thy part and ye shall be greatly rewarded - I say ye shall be rewarded And too I say - we do stand ready to give unto thee as ye are prepared to receive -- So be it our part to prepare thee after ye have done thy part So be it we do not betray ourself or our trust -- Be ye blest of me and of my presence ---

I am thy Sibor and thy Brother - Sananda - Son of God

Sister Thedra of the Emerald Cross

One Hand Serves the Other

Bor speaking:

Beloved of my being: Blest art thou - blest have ye been-- Ye now have been prepared for the next step - ye now have been brot before the great White Altar - ye have now seen with thy own eyes that which they shall see when come they which are privileged such ---

I say ye have stood upon holy soil - ye have seen with thy own eyes that which is and shall be -- I say it has been and shall remain for them which follow thee -- I say ye are not the first to come and ye shall not be the last -- Lose not the memory of this day - for blest shall ye be ---

I say ye have been blest - and ye shall now bring with thee thy physical body - and ye shall bring with thee one other - and ye shall be as one prepared to stay within this place for a period of time - and ye shall be as one prepared for a part which shall be given thee to do ---

Blest are they which do come unto this altar -- I say ye shall be true unto thyself and keep for thyself that which is for thee - and give unto them that which is for them - and ye shall have for them an abundance yet ye shall break no law ---

Ye shall bless them as ye have been blest - and they shall be unto thee that which shall be unto thee my hand and my foot - they shall bless thee in turn ---

I am with thee - yet they shall do thy bounties and they shall be thy helpers - they shall be of service unto thee - and they shall be unto thee the other hand - with joy and thanksgiving shall they serve ---

I am thy Sibor and thy Brother -

Sister Thedra of the Emerald Cross

See Beyond the Mask of Flesh

Sanat Kumara speaking into thee of understanding -- Ye shall be as one prepared for the "Greater Part" - and ye shall say unto them in my name and as I would say - that "there are none so foolish as the one which thinks himself wise - and none so sad as the one which betrays himself"---

Now I say - ye shall be of a mind to learn that which has been given unto thee - and when this is learned ye shall be led into a new field of learning - ye shall receive great and wonderous revelations of the NEW AGE ---

It is now come when new laws shall be revealed unto them which have been true unto themself and have learned the lessons well ---

I say ye are not alone - nor shall ye walk alone - for ye shall be as ones which have my hand upon thee - and ye shall be as ones prepared for that which shall be given unto thee to do - ye shall be as ones prepared for the next step ---

There is no other eternity other than this hour - it is omnipresent - and this day is the only day ye shall ever know! for there are no tomorrows - and yesterday exists only in thy memory -- Be ye as one which can apply thyself this day unto thee - and ye shall do well to study the law well - and to ponder upon that which has been written.

I say ye shall determine this day thy course - and pity are they which are turned aside - for they shall begin anew -- Blest are they which do attain ---

Be ye as ones mindful of thy benefactors and ye shall draw them near unto thee - and ye shall be glad for them -- I am come that ye may be brot out of bondage - and ye shall be blest of me and by me -- Be ye alert for one shall walk in thy midst unknown unto thee -- When they have passed thy way ye shall wonder at thy slowness - be ye as one which can see beyond the mask - beyond appearance - for it shall be revealed unto thee one has walked in thy midst - and masked shall he be ---

I say - be ye not deceived by appearance - for he shall wear a mask not of paper but of flesh -- See him for that which he is - and be ye not concerned with his appearance - for he comes from afar - with feet sore and weary - and ye shall give unto him food when it is come - and ye shall bless him - and let him go in peace -- Be ye blest by him and of him ---

I am Sanat Kumara

Sister Thedra of the Emerald Cross

The Great Psychiatrist

Sananda speaking: -

Beloved of my being: Be ye blest of me and by me and I come that ye may be blest - I come that ye may have great light---

I give unto thee one law this day - and it is: Be ye at peace within thyself - follow in the way I set before thee - and give unto thyself credit for being a Son of God -- And bother not for the trivialities which beset thee - ye have within thy hand the key unto the Kingdom and ye know it not --

Be ye as one at peace with thy soul and ye shall bless thyself -- I can but point the way and set thy feet upon the path - and when ye have been shown the way ye alone can walk in it - blest are they which walk therein ---

While ye are within the world of men ye see not the plan - ye know not the fullness thereof - yet ye are as ones which have a part which is necessary unto the whole -- Be ye as ones prepared to pick up thy cross and follow me - and I shall lead thee into the way which is new and strange unto thee - and ye shall be as one which has earned thy passport into strange and new places -- Many things shall be revealed unto thee and ye shall be glad ---

I am one sent of God that ye may be found and brot in - and that ye might be prepared - and ye shall do that which is necessary to prepare thyself for that which is to be done - and ye shall be as one joyful of heart and glad for all thy trials and temptations ---

I say ye shall overcome all things and ye shall arise above the way of the uninitiated - ye shall seek thy freedom from bondage -- Ye shall <u>work</u> for thy freedom - ye shall s<u>eek</u> it from the Source -- Ye shall go into the secret place and examine thyself and find that which is thy torment and cleanse it from thee and remember it no more - give it no lodging place and give it no power over thee ---

I say thy own discomforts are as nothing compared to the torment of one consumed of his wonton ---

I say - be ye of a mind to learn - and I shall give unto thee greater things -- I give not the pearls of great price unto babes which know not their worth -- I am with thee unto the end ---

I am thy Sibor and thy Brother - Sananda - Son of God

>   **Sister Thedra of the Emerald Cross**

Fashion for Thyself the Garment Ye Shall Wear Tomorrow

Sanat Kumara speaking: -

Be ye blest of me and by me - for I come that ye may be blest -- Ye shall give unto them this word that they may know that which I say unto thee - they shall bear witness of these my words - and they shall have within them the comprehension of that which is said --

Now for the first time I say unto thee: Ye have given of thyself that they might receive that which is given unto thee - and they have as yet received nought else than thru thy grace - and they are not mindful of thee - I say they are not mindful of thee -- They are not given unto thotfulness and they are given unto the pettishness which besets them - They are as ones filled with little things - they have not forsaken them they are as yet not prepared for the next step -- I say they give unto themself credit for being wise - they carry their weapons of defense as they go in and out -- I say they come in on the defensive - they go out on the defensive - they are as ones ready to defend themself and that which they have brot into the temple with them -- They leave not their smallness nor their pettishness behimd - they ask of themself counsel -

they give unto themself credit for being wise - I say they have a way to go -- Be ye as one which has my hand upon thee and ye shall not be deterred from thy way nor shall ye stumble - I say ye shall stumble not.

I say we are mindful of thee - we have not found thee wanting -- We are not as one which forsake our own - be ye of good countenance And now ye shall be as one which has thy hand in mine and I shall lead thee - and I shall give unto thee that for which ye have waited ---

Now ye shall give unto them this part individually - and they shall ponder it and they shall not make of me a fool nor shall they call me a liar -- I am not blind - nor do I betray myself - I see - I hear - there are no doors closed against me - yet I enter not into the places wherein they turn against me ---

I say - when they turn against me I enter not ---

Be ye as ones which have the mind to comprehend these my words and ye shall learn that which is said in secret shall be revealed openly - there are no secrets - only thy own unknowing -- Fashion for thyself the garment ye shall wear tomorrow - fashion for thyself this day thy dwelling place tomorrow - and ye shall be the creator of each and every garment and each and every dwelling place ---

Be ye either true or traitor -- I say - be ye true unto thyself - and give unto thyself credit for being a Son of God - and walk in the way set before thee - ask of no man his opinion - keep thy own counsel - and be ye as one which has within thy hand the key - ye have but to turn it -- It is clearly written and recorded within the laws herein recorded for all which do have eyes to see -- Be ye as one which can see - be ye not blinded by that which would hold thee fast- and that which would bind thee in the world of darkness -- I am come unto thee that ye may be blest - and when ye accept me ye accept my ambassador my messenger in my name - and I have spoken and ye have heard me - I am and I know myself to be Son of God -- So be it -- Amen and Selah

Sister Thedra of the Emerald Cross

Whoredom

Sanat Kumara speaking: -

Blest be ye this day -- Thy eyes shall behold the glory of God - praise ye His Holy name -- Sing ye the songs - O ye - all the nations of the Earth -- Lift up thy eyes - see ye the glory of the heaven - look unto the heaven for thy salvation - for it lies not in the Earth - for ye have desecrated her - and all that ye have created within her have ye created like unto the whore - ye have created like unto the unjust and the foolish.

Ye have builded temples of stone and mortar - ye have colored them with the blood of Saints -- Ye have martyred thy Saints and named thy temples for them ---

Ye have gone the long way to give unto thyself credit for being wise. O ye fools - ye babble of thy knowledge - of thy wealth and of thy love and of thy mercy -- Ye fools! I say this is the day of accounting when ye shall be caught up short of thy course - ye shall be found wanting - ye shall be brot face to face with thy foolishness ---

Now it is recorded and wisely so - that there are none so sad as the one which betrays himself or his trust -- Now it is come that ye shall reap what ye have sown and reap ye shall - I say ye shall reap as ye have sown - and ye shall be as one which has sown unto the whorl* wind ---

I am come that justice may prevail - I say justice shall prevail - the law shall be served in all lands - in all places of the Earth - and in all the firmaments of the heavens shall it prevail -- I say justice shall prevail in all the lands of the Earth - and none shall escape the law - and he which would try is the greatest of fools ---

I address myself to the fools which think themself wise - which do plunder the temples of God - which desecrate the written word - which try to besmirch the servants of God - the ones which do send forth thy youth into battle in the name of God -- I say – O ye fools! heed these my words: Ye shall be brot to justice - ye shall give an accounting of all thy ways - ye as shall be unto thyself judge - ye shall gnash thy teeth with fear and trembling at the mighty power of God - which has sent thee out from Him - ye shall fall on thy face and cry out in judgement ye shall call for mercy - and ye shall find none - pity shall ye be ---

I now speak unto my servants - for I am come that ye may be spared the great and terrible day -- I say unto thee: Be ye as ones prepared for that which shall come upon the Earth - and they which are true unto themself and their trust shall be caught up with the Mighty Host -- For it is near time when there shall be a new port which shall draw nigh unto the Earth - whereupon shall be the Heavenly Host - and they shall pass near unto the Earth - and the ones which are prepared shall be gathered together and brot in as ones so prepared -- And upon that port ye shall be as ones prepared for the great day - when each and every one shall be removed from the surface of the Earth -- I say - ye which are the remnant shall be caught up with the host - which has been referred to as the Royal Assembly - and prepared for the task which shall be allotted unto thee -- Ye shall return unto the Earth as man - ready to do that which shall be given unto thee to do -- Ye shall choose that which ye shall do and then ye shall be given instruction in thy part and returned fully qualified to do it - such is wisdom -- Be ye at the altar tomorrow for further enlightenment ---

I am thy Sibor and thy Brother - Sanat Kumara

Sister Thedra of the Emerald Cross

*Whorl = that which pertains to imperfection

Comprehend the Laws

Sarah speaking:-

Sori Sori Sori O my children: Praise the name of Solen - give Him all the praise and the glory forever and forever -- Be ye blest of me and by me - I am thy mother eternal - and I shall be unto thee that which thy Father God would have me be - and I shall be unto thee the breath which ye breathe ---

I shall be unto thee the life which ye are - for from me have ye gone out -- I say ye have had thy being in me - thru me and with me - and ye have forgotten me -- I say ye shall now remember me and return unto thy rightful estate and ye shall be glad for thy remembering ---

Bless this day and give thanks for all thy trials and temptations - and rise with me - soar with me -- Come my children with me into the realm where peace abides - rest thy weary head upon my breast - leave behind thy little worries - thy small and trivial cares - thy puny talk and thy words which are sent into the eth so heedlessly - with no thot of that which they bring back unto thee ---

Be ye as ones which can comprehend that which I say unto thee - and I shall draw thee nigh unto me - and I shall cause thee to hear my voice and I shall speak unto thee in the hours of thy sleep - and I shall cause thee to be quickened - and thy memory shall be returned unto thee - and for this have ye waited -- Blest are they which do receive their memory - I come that ye may have it so ---

Be ye as ones which can go from this altar this day with my hand upon thee - walk with me -- Hear me O my children - for I am near unto thee even as thy hand and foot - give thanks and be glad - give thot unto that which has been said unto thee let it not pass from thee so easily.

Be ye as ones which can comprehend the laws set down for thy own welfare - fear not and be ye as ones responsible for thy own preparation for ye alone can come - none shall bring thee unprepared ---

Cleanse thy heart - thy hand - and be ye as ones prepared to receive him which shall come - he will not be deceived nor is he so foolish as to give unto the unprepared the pearl without price - I say he shall give unto thee nought until ye have prepared thyself for to receive it ---

Be ye blest of him and ye shall be glad for thy preparation -- So be it ye shall call out and ye shall be heard and answered - I am with thee unto the end ---

I am thy Mother - Sarah

Sister Thedra of the Emerald Cross

Lift Up Thine Eyes

Sanat Kumara speaking unto thee: -

Beloved of my being: I come unto thee this day that ye may be given that which has been kept for thee - and it is for the good of all mankind that I come ---

Now ye shall say unto them in my name - that they shall be as ones which have the law given unto them which is given unto US -- I say we which have gone before thee to prepare the way before thee have followed these laws - or the <u>one</u> <u>law</u> to the letter - we break it not - for we have the wisdom of the initiate -- I say - ye have been given the key to the Kingdom of God - if ye will but see it ---

I say: Will ye not walk in the path set before thee? - and ye shall be glad forevermore -- Rejoice that it is now come when these things shall be revealed unto thee - and ye shall be glad thruout all eternity that ye have been delivered out ---

Now it is come when great stress shall come upon all the peoples of the land - and they shall fall under the yoke of oppression - and I say unto thee my people: Lift up thine eyes unto the hills - lift up thy heart unto the everlasting Shrine - which is thy own light within the Inner Temple wherein ye shall go - wherein all things shall be revealed unto thee ---

I say this is the Royal Road upon which ye have come -- I say ye are now entering into the portals of learning - and ye know not what lies ahead of thee - and ye see not beyond the veil -- Ye go in and out from thy place of abode with no vision of that which is to come - ye are blinded by the veil of Maya -- Yet my people! Lift up thine eyes and open up thy heart - and ye shall be touched and quickened - and ye shall comprehend the law - and ye shall walk with surety - and with dignity and ye shall not make a mockery of that which has been given unto thee for thy own welfare ---

I say ye shall not mock me - ye shall not make a mockery of the law set down before thee - ye shall not give unto me the bitter cup -- Ye shall not persecute my prophets - ye shall bless them - and give unto them as they would give unto thee -- Ye shall give unto them food and drink - for they are sent unto thee even as I am sent - for as I receive of God the Father - so do I give unto them and they in turn give unto thee.

I am now come that there might be great light among thee O my people - be ye alert and hear me! for I am come that ye may be delivered out before the great day of sorrow - I come that ye might be up and about thy preparation - that ye might be brot out of bondage --

HEAR ME - HEAR ME! ALL YE PEOPLE OF THE EARTH! - I stand ready to give unto thee as ye are prepared to receive - and I say - ye have received little - yet my store is boundless - and ye comprehend not the fullness of the Father's House -- Arise and come home - O ye children of Earth - ere the great day of sorrow!

I am thy older Brother and thy Sibor - Sanat Kumara

Recorded by Sister Thedra

Remember What has been Said

Beloved of my being: Be ye blest of me and of my presence -- I come that ye may be blest - I give unto thee power and the authority to say unto them in my name that they shall be as ones brot out of bondage - and they shall walk in the way set before them -- With great joy and dignity shall they walk - and they shall faint not - nor shall they weary of well doing - for it is near time when great trials and temptations shall beset the peoples of the Earth -- Ye shall not be alone in thy trials and in thy longings - I say unto thee - thy longings shall be great indeed -- And shall ye not find they strength within thy being - which is thy eternal being - which is thy self unveiled ---

Be ye as one which can hold fast unto the Light of the Christ which never fails - and I say unto thee - ye shall find strength and peace which ye have not remembered -- Bear in mind that which has been said unto thee - and ye shall find the strength which will surpass all thy knowing Blest are they which hold fast in the time of trials and temptations ---

I say ye shall be as ones alert and watchful - for too I say - ones do walk among thee which would torment thee - and take from thee thy peace of mind -- I say unto thee: Hold fast unto the law - walk ye in the way set before thee - and ye shall find strength therein and ye shall be given the comprehension of the Saints - which now walk among thee.

I say that thy martyred Saints are now within physical form - they do walk among thee - veiled tho they be -- I say - the ones ye have called great - and near great - the ones which have suffered that ye may follow in the path which they have found - that ye might live in the temples they have founded - that ye might have the laws revealed - that ye may be brot out of bondage - I say unto thee - these are now within physical bodies - and they are prepared to reveal themself unto the just and the prudent -- I say ye shall prepare thyself for great revelation - and too I say - ye shall receive as ye are prepared -- So be it and Selah.

I am with thee that ye may be enlightened of God the Father -- So be it my part to give unto thee as ye are prepared to receive ---

I am thy Sibor and the Brother - Sanat Kumara

Recorded by Sister Thedra

Sibor - Master - Disciple

Bor speaking:- Beloved of my being: I come at this time that I might bear witness of thy integrity -- I say unto thee: Thy hands are clean - thy heart is pure - I say unto thee: ye have been true unto thyself - ye have kept thy own counsel - ye have gone the long way to bless them - ye have given unto them that which is for them - and kept for thyself that which is given unto thee -- I say ye have been faithful in all things and ye shall be as one which has proven thyself trustworthy - and ye shall go out from the place wherein ye are as one prepared for the greater part ---

Now I shall speak unto them which are fortuned to read these my words: There are many called and few are chosen - and they which are chosen are chosen as ones which have qualified themself thru the ages past - they have labored long for their reward - and they have earned the right to call themself "Sibor" "Master" and "Disciple" - they qualified for each part -- I say that even the disciple prepared himself to become a disciple of the Masters - he has given himself - he has brot his hands - his heart - and surrendered up himself for that which the Master has given unto him ---

In like manner does the Master surrender up himself unto his Sibor and so on -- He has the will to learn of his instructors - he has the mind and he does not speak spiteful – nor does he cast suspicion upon his so-called 'instructor' - he gives his love and his attention - he has been prepared for the part of di<u>sci</u>ple ---

And now I say with my Brothers - that as ye are prepared so shall ye receive - ye shall choose this day that which ye shall do -- And when it is come that one shall walk among thee as one prepared to give unto thee the 'Water of Life' - I pray that ye may be prepared to receive him and of him ---

I say - this is thy own preparation - and the law has been set before thee - ye have been fortuned this part - this knowledge - and ye have the gift of f<u>re</u>e w<u>ill</u> - and ye shall either accept or reject it -- But let it be recorded that when it is given unto thee freely and it is rejected - ye shall begin at the beginning -- I say - sad is the one which does betray himself - pity is he! Blest is he which does receive of the Water of Life for he shall be forever free -- So be it and Selah --

I am come that ye might be alert - and that ye might see and hear - that ye may k<u>no</u>w - and ye have to be thy own judge - which is the way ye shall choose - none shall trespass on thy f<u>re</u>e w<u>ill</u> -- I speak unto thee frankly and fearlessly - and I am responsible for that which I say - and none shall suffer for that which I say - and none shall suffer for that which I have said or done -- I am not of a mind to see my sibets suffer for my sake - yet I have said things for thy own sake which should alert thee -- I am the father of discipline - so be it that I am thy Brother sent of the Father and the Mother Eternal - I am Bor

Recorded by Sister Thedra

THE GATE IS GUARDED WELL

Blest art thou this day - and blest shall ye be - for I come that this day shall bear fruit -- I give unto thee of myself that ye may be blest as I have been blest of the Father Mother God - and ye shall come to know me even as I know the Father Mother ---

My dear children: For thy chidings art thou stronger - and wiser shall ye become -- I say unto thee - I am not of a mind to sibor the wanton and the willful - yet I shall plant thy feet upon a hill - I shall place within thy hand a key - which ye shall turn at will - and ye shall be as one prepared to enter into the temple gate ---

I say unto thee: The gate is guarded well - and the gate stands threefold - and the temple is four square -- And ye shall find the center thereof and mark it well - for therein shall be thy abiding place -- Ye shall put out thy hand and I shall touch thee - and I shall quicken thee - and ye shall remember that which ye have done and said in the days of thy forgetting---

I say ye shall remember all that which ye have forgotten - such is wisdom -- I say the temple is sealed - and now it shall be unsealed - and ye shall stand as ones unveiled - thy frontpiece shall be removed - and ye shall be unbound - and ye shall stand forever free and ye shall be glad -- So be it and Selah---

Praise the Father Mother which has sent thee out as themself - ye are ONE with them -- Only in thy unknowing have ye separated thyself from them - and ye have had thy memory blanked from thee - yet I say ye shall have it returned unto thee - such is the Will of the Father Mother God -- So be it and Selah---

I am thy older Brother and thy Sibor - Sanat Kumara -- So be it and Selah --

Recorded by Sister Thedra

The Call Goes Out: Sori Sori Sori

Blest be ye this day for I am with thee -- O My Children: Ye are blest as none other - thine is a part different from all others - in no age have they had that which is fortuned unto thee -- O My Children - lift up thy hearts - raise up thy heads - Hear Me! HEAR YE ME! I speak unto thee from the depth and from the heights - I cry unto thee -- O YE CHILDREN OF ALL THE LANDS OF THE EARTH - HEAR ME!

I come that ye may <u>not</u> go down into utter darkness -- O ye - my beloved children - long have I waited this day -- I say unto thee: This is the day for which I have waited - that ye might return unto me -- Be ye as ones which have ears to hear me - and a mind to learn - and give unto me thy hand - and no harm shall come near unto thee -- I say I shall bring thee out of bondage forever- and no darkness shall consume thee -- My children - I have said unto thee at this altar - that I shall bring thee out as ye are prepared - so be it - and I ask of thee nought save that ye may learn of me*-- It is necessary to give unto me thy heart - thy hand - and surrender up thyself for all thy opinions shall avail thee nought ---

I say - ye shall come unto me void of thy preconceived ideas - and void of opinions -- I say ye know me not! and ye can find me in the temple wherein ye shall come - I say - within the place wherein I am ye shall find me ready to receive - and I shall welcome thee home ---

I say unto thee my children: Of all the lands of the Earth - I have not turned thee away -- Ye have forgotten me - long have ye gone from me - and ye have not had the mind to return unto me ---

I say unto thee - ye shall now give thot unto me - and ye shall ponder my words - and I shall reveal myself unto thee - and ye shall be glad! Great shall be thy revelations - and great shall be thy joy!

I am with thee and I am glad! So be it I shall watch thy progress and I shall speak unto thee many times - and ye which are of a mind - shall receive me in the name of the Most High Living God -- So be it and Selah ---

I am thy Mother Eternal - Sarah

Recorded by Sister Thedra

*"Pearls without price" - "Priceless my gems"

The One to Come - Mother Sarah

Sarah speaking: -

Beloved Child which is my hand made manifest unto them: Blest art thou and blest shall ye be -- Be ye as my voice unto them and say unto them in my name - and as I would have thee say - that one shall come unto thee from out the great Cosmos - from out the heart of God the Father shall he come - and he shall take upon him a body of flesh - a body of flesh and bone - and he shall be as one come for the first time.

I say he has not had the body of flesh and bone - he has not gone into darkness - nor shall he - for he shall be as one sent of the Father - and he shall not have his memory blanked from him - for he shall remember all that he IS - and all that he shall ever BE - he shall know he shall walk among thee as one prepared for this day ---

He shall walk as one which has all power - and as one prepared to give unto them as the Father made incarnate upon the Earth -- I say great is this day - and great IS this day!

I say the heavens shall open up its doors - and they which are so prepared shall have free concourse into all the places thereof ---

I say ye shall prepare thyself for that which is yet to come -- I say ye shall be as ones prepared for that which shall come upon the Earth - Too I say - ye shall see the fulfillment of all the prophecies which have been given for this time - for there shall be great and trying times - when the waters shall flow upward - and the fire shall mingle with the water - and the thorn shall grow on the wheat - and the rose shall bloom from the oak ---

I say ye shall live to see prophecy fulfilled - and for this shall ye prepare thyself -- Ye shall bless this day when ye have received me - and of me - for I shall send one out from the place of my abode - which shall gather them in which are so prepared - and they shall be gathered as the hen gathers her chicks - Be ye as one on whose shoulders rests the responsibility of that which shall be given unto thee to do -- I say each shall play his part - and for this shall he prepare himself -- And ye shall not fall - nor shall ye falter - for I say unto thee - I SHALL WALK WITH THEE AND I SHALL SUSTAIN THEE ---

PEARLS are my children - and JEWELS are my thots - and few are prepared to receive my JEWELS - and not one of my PEARLS shall go unaccounted for - for they are numbered - one by one - I know each by name - and I see them wherever they be - and I have suckled them at my breast - and I hold them close that they may not go in deep sleep -- I nourish them and I give unto them as they are prepared to receive -- I say I do not waste time or energy in vain - I am the Mother eternal and I know them which sleepeth - and them which are awake - and I too know them which are beginning to stir from their slumbers ---

Now it is come when many shall awaken - and they shall be glad it is over - for it is given unto me to know that which has bound them in the hours of their unknowing - in the time of their sleep -- Now they shall call out and they shall be heard and answered - and they shall be blest indeed - and they shall be brot in and refreshened and purified - such is the will of the Father ---

I ask of thee nothing more than accept my love and my hand - and I shall bring thee into the place wherein I am - and I shall rejoice with thee that it is finished - Praise the name of Solen forever and forever - for He has given unto thee being - and He has given of Himself that ye might be - and He has willed that ye return unto Him this day --- So be it - and I am thy Mother Eternal - Sarah

Recorded by Sister Thedra

The Emerald Cross

The Cross - it is a Company - an Order of beings who work within the Brotherhood of Man and the Fatherhood of God - for the good of all mankind ---

And at the head of this group one known as Mother Sarah - the personification of Love - embodiment of all Mothers - that is: The Love of God the Father made <u>manifest</u> <u>in</u> <u>mothers</u> -- The blessed Mother Sarah is the Head of this Order of The Emerald Cross ---
And when one earns the Divine right and privilege to associate themself with this Order - it is the joy of all the Orders and Brothers of Light -- I speak for the Order - for I am one known as Merseda ---

Spoken to Sister Thedra of The Emerald Cross

Emanations of Deity

Born speaking: -

I speak unto thee from out the emanations of Deity - I speak unto thee from the fullness of eternity - I call unto thee from the depth - from the heights -- I speak of Spirit - I speak of flesh - I speak of that which eternally is - and that which changeth not -- I speak unto thee of that which shall - and does change - I speak of c<u>hang</u>e and change is good and shall be good ---

And no man shall stay the hand of Deity -- I say - no man shall change the LAW - for it is the law that all things or within the realm of matter be changed - there is no staleness within the realm of spirit -

spirit is the newness of all things made pure -- I say: All things which are within the realm of matter shall be changed - cleansed and made pure - such is the law --

I say - such is the law of the Great and Grand Spirit - Father Mother God - which has called forth all manifestation which is made manifest I say - all that is now made manifest shall be returned unto Spirit and made fresh - made pure.

I say it is the law which is given unto all the lands - all the countries all planets - all galaxies - all peoples within and on all planets - all galaxies thruout the systems of all creation - all that which is created and that which shall be created ---

Now ye shall speak unto them in my name and as I would - that I come unto them from out the heart of God the Father - I come as His emanation that He has willed - that He has sent out as His pulsation - as His breath -- And I would speak unto thee as a Brother which as yet has not taken upon Self the body of flesh and bone ---

I have not spoken as man - I have not spoken as one of Earth - I have not been born of woman - yet I AM -- I am unborn of Earth - yet I shall take embodiment thru woman upon Earth - as Earth shall I be born -- I say unto thee - I shall be born of woman - in the same manner as was thy Lord - known unto thee as Jesus the Christ - known unto us as Sananda Son of God ---

I say - in like manner shall I be born -- I say - one has been prepared as was the Mother Mary of Jesus thy Lord - the Master Sananda ---

I say - one has been prepared even as she - that she may receive me. As a child of twelve I shall make my entrance into the world of man -

and therein shall I walk and talk -- I shall bring with me a legion of the realms of light - I shall have a place prepared for to receive me - and I shall have a place within the land wherein ye are at this time -- I say the place is there - and it is now being prepared - and it is guarded well -- And I say there are great preparations being made to receive me - and the hosts which I shall bring with me -- And when I shall go out I shall be as no man has been - I shall be different from all others ---

I shall carry with me a blue star and all which look upon it shall know me - and they shall be gathered into the place wherein I am - wherein I shall be at that place - wherein I shall abide - and they shall become part of the host which I shall have with me ---

I say ye shall prepare thyself - for ye know not that which is to be - that which shall come upon the Earth -- I say - great revelation is in store for thee - and great shall be the day ahead -- Blest shall ye be - and blest art thou -- Blest shall they be which endureth to the end ---

I am BORN

Recorded by Sister Thedra

The Time of Stress

Sanat Kumara speaking: -

Be ye blest of me and by me - for I come that ye may be blest -- Ye have given unto me great joy - for ye have overcome that which has been unto thee a great and heavy cross - ye have been true unto thyself and ye have held thy peace - and ye have given unto thyself credit for knowing which way to go -- Ye have gone the way set before thee - ye have given of thyself that they may be blest - ye have faltered not - nor have ye stumbled -- I say ye have done well - I say ye shall be blest -- So be it and Selah ---

Now let it be recorded that there shall be a mighty wind - and it shall be unto thy place of abode -- Many there shall be which shall look for a place to lay their head - and they shall be given the place - and they shall be as ones which have with them the children which shall be comforted in the time of stress-- So be it and Selah -- I say ye shall comfort them in the time of stress - such is my word unto thee - for I have spoken and ye have heard me -- So be it and Selah --

I am thy older Brother - Sanat Kumara

Recorded by Sister Thedra

Love in Action

Beloved: I speak unto thee as one which has my hand upon thee - and I say ye shall be blest of me and by me - and I say ye shall speak unto this one as I would - and ye shall speak as I would in Love - for I AM LOVE - I move in the Spirit of Love - I say: I AM LOVE IN ACTION I say I am come that all men may come to know me - and as they receive me - so shall they receive the Father ---

I say I AM COME - I walk in thy midst - and I speak unto them which have prepared themself for to receive me ---

I go not into the places of the dragon for entertainment - I play a lone hand! I am not deceived by appearances! I am not deceived by words - for I know what prompts them! I am not deceived by anything for I am not a fool - neither do I sibor fools -- I speak fearlessly and wisely - I speak out of compassion for the foolish - for they are as the little ones - they know <u>not</u> how short the time left for their preparation I say Life is Life! no beginning - no end - ye shall remember this: "NO END" death is an illusion - no escape from the law! As ye set it into motion it shall fill its cycle and return - all thy joy - all thy torment! Pity are they which set into motion that which shall torment them - I say they betray themself - they shall be as ones which have thrown overboard their own life-belt! So be it I have spoken and I am not finished! I am thy Master - thy Sibor thy Brother which has gone before thee to prepare the way - so be ye wise to walk in it -- I am the Nazarine Sananda - Jesus Christ

Recorded by Sister Thedra

Each unto His Own Part
The Hundred and Forty-Four

Sarah speaking: -

Beloved of my being: Blest art thou and blest shall ye be-- Ye have gone out from me as one which has gone into the Earth for a part which is thine -- All which are within the Earth at this time have certain parts each unto his own and no two are equal - alike - for it is as thy fingerprints - no two alike -- And for the first time I speak unto thee on this subject - and it is for thee to give unto them which are of a mind to learn---

I say - give this unto them which are of a mind to learn-- There are many within the Earth at this time which have parts in the great and divine plan - and no two are alike for they are "parts" - no one has the whole part - and each unto his own -- I say each has been given a part and many have not as yet awakened unto his part -- And too - let it go on record that each is prepared for his part from the beginning of his going out - yet some sleep and are as the traitor - he betrays himself - he thinks himself w<u>is</u>e and he turns from his appointed course - for this does he pay the price - I say he pays a pretty price - he ransoms himself from his own prison - he ransoms himself from the self-created hell - he ransoms himself from his own bondage---

Poor in spirit is he which turns aside from his appointed course -- Now when they which go out as ones called from the Hiarchi they are given "parts- and <u>entruste</u>d with certain parts - and as they prepare themself there are greater parts entrusted them -- And when they have been found worthy they are brot into the place wherein there are treasures untold - wherein they sit in council as "one"- and wherein there is a hundred and forty four of the learned - which are of the Royal Assembly -- And these which make up this Council are as the ones which have thy records -- And nothing is overlooked - nothing hidden and no one is judge of another - the record is the judge -- I say - they which are called shall answer and they shall stand before this tribunal as the initiate which has prepared himself for this part ---

Now it is come when one from among thee shall walk among thee and he shall find them which are prepared to be brot in before the Royal

Assembly - and they which are brot in shall be as ones which have prepared themself in advance ---

I say the path is narrow and strait - I say ye have the key unto the gate - be ye as ones prepared for the greater part-- Praise ye the Lord of Hosts - for mighty is His name -- Praise ye His name all ye people of the Earth ---

I am thy Eternal Mother - Sarah

Recorded by Sister Thedra of the Emerald Cross

The Condition Known as Sleep

Sanat Kumara speaking unto thee of a condition known unto us as sleep When one is in lethargy he sleeps for a time - and awakens within the body of flesh refreshed from his labors -- And when he has refreshed himself he has a clear mind and a poised body -- And when he has a poised body and a clear mind he is receptive to the greater learning - to revelation - and he is as one of a mind to learn - he has the will to learn.

When he is asleep he neither has the mind or the will - hence we refer to them as the "sleepers" - they belong to the sleepers' realm - I say they are asleep! and they have not the mind to learn - nor the will.

Such is the mind of many which are as ones which go and come in the world of man - I say they are of the sleepers' realm and they care not to awaken -- And too I say - should the Lord and Master Jesus Christ Sananda Son of God walk among them this day and speak unto them as he does speak unto thee - and unto all his servants which do serve him on their behalf - they would crucify him this day - they would spit upon him - and they would think upon new ways to torture him -- I say the mind of the beast is in them - I say they are not as ones prepared to receive him - and surely not prepared for the inmost place of the Most High Living God ---

Ye shall say unto them in my name - and with the authority which is mine: I am now prepared to come out from the place wherein I am - as one fully qualified to give unto them as they are prepared to receive I say as they are prepared so shall they receive ---

I am not so foolish as to waste my energy on the foolish - for I have spoken for lo these many days that it is now time to be at thy posts of duty - up and about thy Father's business - and I find them as ones forching upon others their own will - their own parts - their own puny words which they have pilfered from yet others ---

I say they know not that the "Day of the Lord" has come-- I say they are to be found prattling as babes - they are to be found in the places of gaming - wherein they indulge their senses of pleasure - they seek pleasure - not wisdom -- I say they seek phenomena - not truth - they are blind as the male mole -- They cry for the things of Earth - they wander to and fro - bound as by their legirons - they cry - Lord! Lord! and they seek him not -- Such is the pity of man this day ---

I say unto thee - weep not for them - turn not - neither to the right nor to the left - but walk ye in the way which ye shall go -- Be ye blest this day and the labor of thy hands shall be blest -- Mighty is the name of Solen Aum Solen - praise Him all ye children of Earth - lift up thy eyes - open up thy hearts and receive of Him thy eternal freedom - blest shall ye be ---

I am thy older Brother - Sanat Kumara

Recorded by Sister Thedra of the Emerald Cross

Sananda: - Hear Me! Hear Me!

Beloved of my being: It is now come when changes shall come about upon the Earth - and thruout thy country shall be much sorrow and unrest -- I say that these changes shall bring unrest and much suffering -- And too I say - that there are none so sad as the ones which betray themself -- And in a short while ye shall see great strands of water wherein are no waters - ye shall see the waters dry up wherein they have been -- Ye shall see great pestilences rise up to torment thee -- Ye shall give these words to them as I say them - for they shall hear that which I say - and they shall not spit upon them -- For they shall live to see the day not far off - when one shall place himself upon the throne which he sets up - and he shall call himself God - he shall decree that they bow unto him and pay him homage - and he shall demand of them human sacrifice - and they shall do his bidding -- Now I say ye shall hear me out for I am not of a mind to sacrifice up my own - I am of a mind to alert thee - yet should ye turn a deaf ear - I am helpless -- I cry unto thee O my children - be ye alert and hear me! I say ye shall have trying times - and ye shall be as ones true unto thyself and ye shall cling unto the Light -- Ye shall ask of the Father - Light and Truth - ask for comprehension - and walk ye in the way set before thee ---

I say that the way of the dragon is a subtle thing - he would deceive thee and cause thee to be befuddled - he would give unto thee the bitter cup - he would divide my sheep and scatter them -- My children! My children! which I call my sheep - I say he would scatter thee - and confuse thee -- I say unto thee - be ye as one which has my hand upon thee and ye shall be led out of bondage - out of darkness - such is my word unto thee -- Hold fast unto the law set before thee and glad shall ye be ---

I am thy Sibor and thy Brother - Sananda - Son of God -- So be it and Selah

"Grieve not for those who fall on the field of service - for theirs is a crown of Glory....

"Know ye not that there are martyred Saints that walk among you uncrowned?

"I am come that ye may have the comprehension to recognize them Were it not for them I would bring thee into the place wherein I am thru levitation - it will be done - thru a closed circle --"

Recorded by Sister Thedra of the Emerald Cross

The Dragon is Bound in His Own Den

Sananda speaking: -

Beloved of my being: My hand is and has been upon thee -- I say I am with thee and I shall not forsake thee - I say I am not of a mind to forsake thee - and I am given unto watchfulness - I see that which goes on about thee ---

I say unto thee - the lash of the dragon's tail is but the ill wind which bloweth the stench from out his nostrils - he has been bound and he has his hands tied and he has no power to touch thee -- And he is now incarcerated within his own den - and he is furious he has no power over thee - for from this day forward shall he be bound - he shall not come near unto thee -- This is my word - my promise unto thee my child -- Dry thy tears and give unto me credit for that which I am - and I say unto thee I am the keeper at the gate - I am thy gate keeper - and I see that no unclean thing enter into this port - I come into this port and I shall keep it clean - that I might use it for the good of all mankind -- So shall it be -- Be ye as one prepared for the greater part and ye shall be glad - so be it a time of rejoicing -- Amen -- So be it and Selah ---

Say unto them that they shall stand as "One" with one mind - one purpose - and they shall be as one which has the mind to serve the will of the Father -- And they shall be as ones ready for that which shall be given unto them to do - they shall be as ones prepared at all times to be called at the midnite hour - for in the time which is near there shall be a great voice ring out thru the Cosmos - and it shall be recognized by all which has alerted themselves and prepared themself for this day ---

I say - they which are asleep shall be as the sleepers - they shall be found dreaming - and their dreams shall torment them - and they shall be as ones confused - and they shall be as ones frightened and without solace ---

I say - they which are of a mind to learn and which are of a mind to follow me shall be alert - and they shall be without confusion - and they shall be as ones which have my hand upon them and I shall lead them with surety and they shall not fall - nor shall they stumble -- I say they shall not stumble and fall - for I am of the Father sent - and I am not of a mind to leave my sheep unto the wolves ---

Blest are they which hold fast unto the law and blest shall they be - I am come that my sheep be not scattered -- Yet they hear the voices of strange masters which they would follow in the time of their confusion I say they are as ones frightened and confused - for the day of sifting is at hand - and they call out in their delirium and they are as ones bound by that which they know not -- They have not the power within their own hand to fight off the beast - they have not the wisdom which is of the Christed ones - that which is of the Father -- Without their knowing they have nought - I say they have nought -- So be it and Selah ---

To <u>know</u> is wisdom - to <u>think</u> is uncertainty - and to think is not to know - I say therein lies the difference between belief and wisdom -- Man's opinions is not the mind of the Father - and it is the tower of Babel which shall fall - it shall crumble at their feet - for they which <u>think</u> themself wise shall be found wanting - I say they shall be brot face to face with their foolishness -- So be it and Selah ---

I am responsible for that which I say - and no man shall call me a fool -- So be it and Selah ---

I am Sananda - Son of God

The One to Come Shall Take Upon Himself the Cross of Flesh

Sanat Kumara speaking: -

Beloved of my being: Be ye as my mouth and as my hand made manifest unto the ones which gather themself together - and say unto them in my name that it is now come when great shall be the activities within the Earth and about it ---

I say we which do sit in council are alert - we have our eyes open and we see and know that which does go on -- And I say with wisdom and with surety - that it is the part of thy guardians to protect thee in the hours of stress -- I say that there are no traitors among us - we speak unto truth and wisdom and we speak fearlessly - for it is given unto us to know the law - and I say we abide by it -- So be it that we walk in the way which we point out unto thee - and I say that we have gone before thee to prepare the way before thee - and ye shall prepare thyself diligently for that which shall be entrusted unto thee to do ---

Now let this go on record - that each has his own free will and none shall trespass upon it -- And when one comes unto thee and inquires of thee - ye shall give unto him the law - and he shall choose that which he shall do with it - he shall be as one free to choose -- He shall be as one wise to choose to abide by it - he shall be as a traitor unto himself to refuse it -- So be it the law - as they ask so shall they receive -- So be it and Selah ---

I say one shall come from out the east and he shall be as no other - and he shall be as one which has taken embodiment thru woman - yet he shall be of light - he shall not be the seed of man - and he shall go out from his place of physical birth at the age of twelve - and he shall walk among thee as God the Father made manifest in flesh -- He has not been born of woman (before) - he has not walked the Earth as man and he has not taken upon himself the cross of flesh -- I say he has not taken upon himself the chemical form of animal man - he has not come into thy realm (before) - he shall - and ye shall be as ones to see him -- I say he shall bring great light - and all which are so prepared shall walk with him and see him face to face - such shall be thy reward -- So be it and Selah ---

I am thy Brother and thy Sibor - Sanat Kumara

Recorded by Sister Thedra of the Emerald Cross

As the Moth Which Goes into the Flame

Sananda speaking: -

Beloved of my being: Ye have said that which I have given unto thee to say - and I speak unto thee as one prepared to give unto thee the "new" part - and it shall be new - separate and unlike any other ---

Ye shall be as one prepared for this part - and I say unto thee - the "old" shall serve thee well - and ye shall bless the day which has been unto thee thy stepping stone -- Ye have gone the long way to bless them and they have not known thee - nor are they of a mind to recognize thee.

I say they shall be as ones awakened unto the Father's work - and they shall be as ones come alive -- I say they shall awaken and they shall come alive - I say they which have my hand upon them shall awaken -- I am not so foolish as to awaken them aforehand - for it is not lawful

They should be as the moth which goes into the flame - they should be as the cocoon which is opened aforetime - I am not unmindful of the law ---

I say - I am mindful of my sheep - and one which is qualified to do the Father's will - thru me it is done -- So be it and Selah ---

Blest shall ye be this day - blest shall they be which come unto this altar - be they blest of me ---

I am Sananda - Son of God

Recorded by Sister Thedra of the Emerald Cross

Born - The Virgin Spirit

Sori Sori Sori --

Be ye blest of me and by me -- I come unto thee from out the great cosmic heart - I bring unto thee great tidings - I bless thee with such tidings that I bring -- I say unto thee: Be ye mindful of that which I am saying unto thee at this time ---

The day is now come when one shall walk upon the Earth in flesh as Spirit made manifest - which is from out the heart of the cosmos - from out the heart of all divinity - and he shall be as God the Father incarnate in flesh -- He shall be a virgin spirit - for he has not taken upon himself a body of flesh and bone - he has not walked among man as such - he has not been as one which has gone out from the Father -

he has not in any form separated himself from the Father - and he shall now go out as man - for the first time shall he go out ---

I say - he shall take upon himself the garment of flesh and bone - he shall walk as man - he shall be as man - yet he shall be as none other for he shall be as God incarnate - he shall be as the living - breathing - pulsating life of God the Father - he shall know himself to be the Father incarnate -- And he shall go into a place which is prepared to receive him - and he shall take upon himself a body of earthly substance thru woman - I say - he shall born of the womb of woman -- He shall be the fruit of woman - yet he shall not be the seed of man - for he shall be born of God the Father - he shall be of light -- He shall be as one which has not gone into darkness - I say he shall be no part of darkness -- He shall be as one which is the perfect man - he shall be as none other -- He shall be born within the land which is called the greatest of all nations - he shall be as one filled with wisdom - and all power shall be his - for he knoweth all things -- And he has the form of man - yet he will be prepared to change it at will ---

Such shall be his knowledge - and he shall be master of all law and all things -- I say unto thee - ye which have ears to hear and eyes to see: Be ye as ones alert and ye shall be given much which has not hitherto been revealed unto thee - lo the eons of time ye have waited - I say - ye have awaited this day when Earth should receive her King -- Be ye blest this day and blest shall ye be -- I am come unto thee this day that ye may be prepared for the greater part ---

I am thy Brother and thy Sibor - Boran

Recorded by Sister Thedra of the Emerald Cross

The King of Glory –
He shall come as a mighty sound -as a mighty trumpet

Berean speaking unto thee: -

This day shall I speak unto thee concerning the coming of the King Ye have been told that the King of Glory shall make His appearance in the time which is near - it is true -- So be it ---

I come unto thee from out the cosmic center of light - I speak in all languages -- I have spoken all languages and I shall - for it is now come when many shall speak unto the Earth children -- As man shall they speak - and in the languages which each people can understand - I say each shall be spoken unto in his own language - that he may understand that which is said unto him ---

I say - we which are of the Hiarchi do speak as we do for a purpose I say it is given in a certain manner for a purpose - and that purpose is not a mystery - for it is the greater part of wisdom -- And when ye have gone the way of the initiate it shall be revealed unto thee ---

I say - ye are an 'impatient people' filled with curiosity and wonderment -- Ye are not patient and kind - ye rush and push thy way into the halls of learning - ye try to absorb thy knowledge from books ye search the scripts and ye look for signs and for confirmation -- Ye look for peace and security - ye find none! Ye are as ones which have been following man -- Ye seek after signs and miracles - ye are as little children chasing bubbles -- I say ye shall now grow to the age of maturity - and ye shall be given as ye are prepared to receive -- I say ye shall engrave upon thy heart that which is said unto thee - and ye shall remember it - for in the days ahead all things shall pass away - and all thy knowledge of these things swept with them - ye have nothing! ye have no thing! and thy security is as nought -- I speak as one which sees and knows - I know for I am one with the Father which has given unto me being - and He has not withheld His wisdom from me -- I say ye shall stand shorn of all thy credentials - of all thy passports - of all thy glory - of all thy wealth which ye have clung to so tenaciously -- Ye shall stand naked - ye shall stand naked!

Ye shall be as ones wealthy indeed which do enrich thy own life with that which we bring -- I say ye shall be as ones rich indeed when ye make of thyself "A Son of God" - ye shall walk as a Son of God the Father - ye shall walk upright - ye shall give of thyself that others might be comforted - ye shall be a lamp unto their feet -- Ye shall heed these my words - mark them well - and engrave them upon thy heart - and they shall not depart from thee ---

I say ye shall listen for the trumpet which shall ring out - it shall sound thruout all the Cosmos - and ye shall awaken as from the dead - Ye shall lift up thy eyes - and ye shall behold the King of Glory - for He shall come in as a mighty sound - as a mighty trumpet - He shall come as a great Light -- He shall come as a Mighty Host - for He shall be as one which has not been seen - - He shall be seen!

And they which are not prepared for this day shall fall upon their face and call out - Lord! Lord! - they shall freeze in their tracks from fright - they shall die of heart failure - they shall run unto a hiding place they shall panic! And I say unto thee - they shall be as ones gone mad.

Ye shall be as ones prepared for this day - for it is not afar off -- It has been said that the Anti Christ is now upon Earth in flesh and bone. It is so - so be it!

We sleepeth not - nor are we unmindful of our children - we are as parents - watchful of the little ones -- We do not tarry with the trivialities - we are about the Father's business -- Such is wisdom ----

I speak unto thee from out the center of the Cosmos that ye may have Light -- I shall speak unto thee again and again -- Be ye blest of me and by me ---

I am Berean

>Recorded by Sister Thedra of the Emerald Cross

Ye are the Microcosm of His Being

Sanat Kumara speaking: -

Be ye as ones blest this day - for from the One I come unto thee as Deity personified in me -- I say I come as one sent of God the Father that ye may be blest -- I say unto thee that one shall walk among thee as man - and he shall be as one sent of God the Father - he shall come in the time which is near and he shall bring with him a mighty host - for he shall come as one of Light -- For it is now come when balance shall be established within the Earth - it shall be established in the firmaments - it shall be established within thee -- For ye are as the microcosm - ye are the breath of the Father - ye are His breath - ye are the microcosm - ye are but the microcosm of His being -- Ye are but His breath crystalized into form - each form ye have taken - and ye are of no part of the nether world ---

Ye are eternally of Him the Father which has given unto thee being ye are His hand and His foot made manifest upon the Earth -- I say unto thee - be ye as ones which can comprehend that which I say unto thee Ye are His hand and His foot - for none other has He -- He has created and that creation shall and does serve Him as thy hand and as thy foot serves thee

I say - He has no other hand and foot except that which He creates He creates as He sees fit - and He cuts off as He sees fit -- I say He casts off that which He creates - for He has within His hand the power to cast off or to create anew -- He has the one and only power - He has the power to give - the power to take - He has the love and wisdom of the Father - and none other has the right to cast off or to take on -- For He has gone out - He has not gone out - He has remained ever the same and yet He is change - ever changeless - yet all changing -- Ye have not the comprehension of His nature at this time - the greatness is beyond thy concept - yet ye shall know - for ye shall come to know the boundlessness of His Love and His Mercy-- Ye shall be as He for ye shall be enfolded in His bosom - He shall hold thee unto Himself and He shall be glad -- I say ye shall come to know Him - the Father - for it is willed by Him that ye return unto Him and be made whole -- So be it and Selah

So be it - and so be it - I am with thee this day and I am glad -- I come that ye may return unto the place of thy going out - and it shall be a great day - there shall be much rejoicing and great gladness -- So be it and Selah ---

I am Sanat Kumara

Recorded by Sister Thedra of the Emerald Cross

Ye are of the Species which have the Brow which shall carry the Star

Sori Sori Sori -- Beloved children: Be ye blest this day - and blest shall ye be -- I come to thee that ye shall walk in the way set before thee -- Ye shall be as one which has my hand upon thee - and ye shall not fall nor shall ye stumble -- I say when ye are of a mind to be led I shall lead thee gladly - and I shall give of myself that ye may not stumble -- I give of my strength - my energy - my love - my wisdom - for I am of the Father sent that ye may know even as I know ---

Yet my children - I say unto thee again - I am helpless to give unto thee before ye have prepared thyself to receive of me and by me -- Ye have within thy own hand the power to reach out and take that which I have - yet I shall have no less -- I say ye have within thy hand the power to reach out and take that which I have and I should not be impoverished thereby ---

I am now prepared to give unto thee as I have received of God the Father - for this has He sent me -- And ye which are as ones bound by conventions - dogmas - creeds - and within thy own opinions - ye are as ones which close me out - ye simply close me out -- I stand and knock - and ye hear me not - I call and ye answer me not ---

I speak gently while ye are sleeping and ye hoar me not - I cry aloud from the mountain tops - I scale the heights and place thereupon my marks - and ye are as deaf and blind - ye recognize them not - ye hear nothing which I say -- I am now prepared to call again - and I shall use the trumpet - for it is now come when ye shall hear! I say ye shall hear and ye shall see - and ye shall be wise indeed to prepare thyself for such as ye shall hear and see - for it is now come when great changes shall come upon the Earth and upon all peoples of the Earth - and woe unto them which are found wanting ---

I say we are not ministers of doom - We are not born of doom - We preach deliverance -- And ye are of a species which have the brow which shall carry the star - and ye have the fortune to be sent from another galaxy - and ye are within the Earth for a part which is being enacted in the eternal scheme of evolution - and of the Earth - and of man - for ye are not alone -- Every planet has life of one kind or another for this are the planets created - such is the wisdom of the Creator ---

There are ones upon the Earth this day which have come from far and distant planets that this age may be brot into its fullness - I say great shall be this age -- So be it and Selah -- Ye have glimpsed the glory which <u>is</u> and which <u>shall</u> <u>be</u> - I say ye shall live to see the Glory of the King! ye shall see Him and ye shall know Him ---

Ye shall be as one wise to prepare thyself that ye might be caught up with Him -- So be it and Selah ---

I am thy Sibor and thy Brother - Sananda

Recorded by Sister Thedra of the Emerald Cross

Born
The Coming of the King

Sananda speaking: -

Beloved of my being: Be ye blest of me and by me - for I come that ye may be blest -- Ye shall now say unto them in my name - that one shall walk among them as man - and he shall be as flesh and bone - yet ye shall be the Father made manifest upon Earth -- He shall be as one which has not been embodied in flesh before --

I say unto thee - he shall be as none other - for he shall come into embodiment for the first time -- His name shall be called "Born" - and he shall be as the son of woman - yet he shall not be the seed of man - He shall be of light - and for this is he prepared to come among thee as man -- He shall wear a coat of skin which shall not be unto him a burden he shall not be bound by it ---

Now ye shall say unto them - that in the time which is near he shall be born in the greatest of all nations -- He shall be as one cloistered until he is of the twelfth year - then he shall go out into the world wherein he shall reign as King Supreme!

I say - he shall reign as King Supreme -- So be it and Selah ---

Now ye shall ask - why is this? where is this? and ye shall be as ones curious -- I say ye shall first seek wisdom - and all thy questions shall be answered -- So be it and Selah ---

I am now prepared to speak unto thee at length concerning his coming - yet ye shall be as ones prepared for the great day when ye shall see him face to face -- So be it and Selah ---

I am thy Sibor and thy Brother - Sananda

Recorded by Sister Thedra of the Emerald Cross

Anti Christs

Blest of the Father art thou - blest of me art thou -- I come of the Father I am of the Father sent that they may have this portion which shall be given unto thee for them -- Ye shall give it unto them and they shall accept it in the name of the Father - Son and Holy Ghost -- Amen and Selah

I am he which was called: "The Way Shower"- yet they which proclaim me know me not - them which know me follow me -- I say they which do no more than proclaim me know me not -- I too say: They which have their hand in mine look not to the left nor to the right they walk which way I point - they argue not the point ---

Such are the blind and the deaf - they see not the way when I point they hear not that which I say - yet they babble on -- I say they cannot find me in books nor can they find me asleep - for it is now come when great shall be the activity within the realms of light -- I say that the shepherds are not asleep - they know each and every lamb - they know the wolves and their hiding places -- I say they lie in wait for the unsuspecting - they lie in wait to ensnare thee - they are cunning and cruel - for they are the anti-christs ---

I say the anti-christs are among thee - and they seek out the ones which are of a mind to be used by them -- They would silence thy voice and tie thy hands - and they would torment thee --- I say ye shall be alert and ye shall be as one about thy preparation - for it is now come when ye shall choose which way ye shall go -- I am come that ye might choose wisely -- I am and I know myself to be Son of God the Father - known as Solen the First and the Last -- I am Sananda

Sananda

There are none without the presence of God - yet few know that presence - and it is said - without that knowing ye have nothing -- I say again: Without thy knowing - ye have nothing - ye are as ones impoverished - and ye are as ones bound - and ye know not by which ye are bound - ye are of the dark in thy blindness ---

I come that ye may be made to see - and to know - and by my grace shall ye see -- I say I shall raise up my hand and ye shall be caused to see - I say I shall speak and ye shall hear - I say ye shall will it so - and so be it ---

I am now prepared to step forth and give unto thee as I have received of the Father which has sent me -- I come unto thee in His name - and I bless thee as He would have me bless thee -- Be ye as ones blest - accept that which I offer thee in His name - and by Him thru me shall ye be brot out of bondage --

Be ye at peace and poise - give unto no man credit for taking it from thee -- Adoni Adomni and Sheloheim Adomni -

Recorded by Sister Thedra of the Emerald Cross

The Power of the Word

Beloved: My hand is upon thee and great shall be thy revelation - for it is now come when great shall be the light which shall flood the Earth - and the ones which are unprepared shall be as the sleepers and the traitors - they shall sleep on - and they which betray themself shall be the saddest of the lot ---

Be ye as one which has the Light which is - always has been - and ever shall be - and ye shall know that which is meant by Light and Truth and ye shall walk by it -- Ye shall be unto thyself true and ye shall bless this day - and ye shall keep it holy - and ye shall have no false gods before Him which has given unto thee being -- And ye shall praise Him and ye shall be unto Him all that He would have thee be -- So be it ye shall glorify Him in the Earth - and ye shall be unto Him His hand and His foot made manifest upon the Earth - and ye shall walk which way He sets before thee -- Ye shall bless them which do speak evil against thee - and ye shall love them for that which they are - and not for that which they do -- Praise ye the name of Solen Aum Solen - the power and the radiation of that power shall go out from Him thru thee - and ye shall radiate that power and vibration which that sound and vibration carries -- I say - it carries great power - and it is the Word and the Word was God - and the Word became manifest - and the manifestation was God and was good -- And so be it and let it be so -- I am and I know myself to be - so be it ---

I am Sananda - Son of God the Father -- Amen

Beloved of my being: Be ye blest of me and by me - and I shall come in and abide with thee -- Be ye at peace and poise - and say unto them that there are none so foolish as them which think themself wise -- And ye shall say unto them in my name that I shall lead them which hear my voice - and which have the mind to follow me -- It is now come when great stress shall be upon all peoples of the Earth - and great shall be thy endurance--

I say - ye which have the will to follow me shall be led with surety and ye shall find the strength which comes not of flesh - yet which is of flesh shall be strengthened from the peace and the poise which is not of Earth -- Celestial songs shall ye sing within thy heart - and great shall be thy peace within a world of men gone nad -- I say the world of men gone mad shall not torment thee -- Look unto the heavens from whence cometh thy blessings and from whence come th thy strength -- Peace and good will for all mankind shall abide within thee and great shall be thy blessings ---

I keep thee this day - and I am not unmindful of that which goes on in the world of man -- So be it that I am at the throne of my Father - prepared to do His bidding - and I come unto thee that ye may know Him as I know Him -- So be it and Selah ---

I am thy Sibor and thy Brother - Sananda

Recorded by Sister Thedra of the Emerald Cross

"The 144" - "The 12"

Sornica speaking unto the concerning the Temple of the Great White Altar -- I say unto thee: The Temple which is and which has been since the days when the Sons of Solitude went into the east to establish a school wherein the secrets of man - the history of man and his beginning upon Earth - and his origin - might be preserved for this day for this age ---

I say it is now come when great shall be the revelation of and unto them which are prepared for such -- I say that all who are found trustworthy - and who have followed the law shall be brot into the temple which is - and was established by the Sons of Solitude - they are the seven which are the directors of certain activities - and they are the 12 -- There are 144 in toto - and these Brothers are within the Temple of the Great White Altar at this time ---

And I say - ye which are as ones alert and true unto thyself shall be given proof of these my words -- And I have given unto thee a key - and ye shall be as ones wise and keep that which I say unto thee for thyself - for it is the better part of wisdom - for in the time which is near one shall come unto thee with a plan and ye shall hear him out -- So be it and Selah ---

I am come that this might be said -- So be it and Selah ---

I am thy Brother - Sornica

Recorded by Sister Thedra of the Emerald Cross

Prayer

Sananda speaking unto thee: -

Be ye blest of me and by me - for I am come that ye may be blest - Ye shall give this unto them and they shall make it their own -- And none shall lay claim unto it for it shall belong to the ones which hold it within their hearts - and none shall take it from them - for it shall be engraven upon their heart -- I speak unto them which shall accept it as their own - and it shall be unto them a shield and buckler in the time of stress -- I say they shall work with this until it becomes their own --

And it shall not be misused or spoken idly - for it is the sayings of the unwise which are the parts of the idolators and the hypocrites -- I say ye shall engrave this part upon thy heart - make it thy own and great shall be thy reward -- So be it and Selah ---

Be ye blest O my child and hear that which I say unto thee -- I would deliver thee out this day - and yet ye would not be as one prepared to enter into my place of abode -- All things are done according to the law -- So be it and Selah ---

Ye shall now take these words which I shall give unto thee as thy own - and engrave them forever upon thy eternal heart:

Beloved Spirit God - Father Mother - which has caused me to be: Send forth Thy radiant Love - Thy Consciousness thru me that I might glorify Thee in the Earth - that all men might be drawn into Thy Light- and receive of Thy Love and Life without limitation ---

I ask of Thee - that all men might know that which is their divine inheritance willed unto them of God the Father -- Thou art the Father Mother God - and unto Thee all the praise and the glory forever and forever - Amen -- So be it ---

I come unto Thee that all mankind might be blest -- Such is my love for them - and such is Thy Will that all men everywhere be brot out of bondage - O Father Mother God - I do give thanks this day for Thy being - that Thou hast seen fit to give unto me being - that I might go forth as Thou would have me -- That I might walk among them as man as woman - I am glad - Give unto me this day the power and energy to wall as Thou would have me -- No other gods shall I have save Thee -

Blest am I - blest O my soul - praise Him which has sent me forth -- Amen and Selah --

Recorded by Sister Thedra of the Emerald Cross

Water divided from the Wine
Salt divided from the Sand

Sorica speaking unto thee: -

Be ye as one blest of me and by me - for it is now come when I shall speak unto thee of things which are new and strange unto thee - and ye shall be given comprehension - for these things are given at this time for the few which shall be given comprehension -- I say that the few which are now prepared shall comprehend - And them which shall be prepared shall be given comprehension - and they shall receive as they are prepared - for in no wise shall they be given that which is unwise or unjust -- I say - they which have ears to hear shall hear - and they which have eyes shall see - for it is near the time for the gathering in - when the water shall be divided from the wine - and the salt shall be divided from the sand -- And the sheep shall be divided from the goats and the servant shall sup with the master - and the lion shall lie down with the lamb - and the goat shall suckle the child - and the wattling shall nest on the water ---

I say ye shall be as one prepared for strange new things - and ye shall be up and about thy Father's business - for ye shall be as ones true unto thyself - for there are none so sad as the ones which betray themself -- So be it that when the drought is ended - it shall be turbulent waters from the north - and sleet shall cover the fields in the dry and parched lands---

I say ye have seen the last days before the end cometh -- I say ye liveth in the last days of the old cycle - ye likewise liveth in the beginning of the new -- And the old shall pass away and all things shall become new - and for this be ye glad -- Sing ye praise that this day is come and that the old is past -- There shall be a glad new day and peace shall reign - and ye shall be as ones which have heralded in this new order -- Ye have gone thru the fire and come thru victorious - and ye shall be glad for thy victory!

Ye which hear these my words shall remember them well - for ye shall be caused to remember them - for ye shall be as ones which shall have thy memory restored unto thee - for this give thanks -- Praise the name of Solen Aur Solen - praise unto the Father Mother God - praise Him all ye of the Earth -- Amen and Selah ---

I am thy Sibor and thy Brother - Sorica

Recorded by Sister Thedra of the Emerald Cross

He Shall Have the Seal of Solomon

Sorica speaking: -

Be ye blest of me and by me - for this do I come -- I speak upon a subject which is new unto thee - I say that which ye have not heard - and which ye have not seen -- I say unto thee that there are great and powerful forces which now surround the place wherein ye are - and these forces are not of Earth nor are they created by man - these forces are for thy protection and for thy welfare ---

I say that the ones which are not prepared for the greater work shall be unable to stand before this power - for great indeed it is! I say that it is indeed great! And they which are prepared for to receive of such strength and power shall be as ones which are prepared to enter into the Temple wherein is the Altar of White Alabaster ---

I say that the Temple wherein stands the White Altar shall be the place of thy great initiation and the place of thy unveiling -- So be it that they which do go out from this temple shall find them which are ready and they shall bring them in -- I say they which have prepared themself shall be brot in - and great shall be their joy -- I say unto them - it is worth all thy effort -- So be it and Selah ---

I speak unto them which are yet in darkness - and they which are afraid and which give unto themself credit for being wise: Ye shall be as ones which have been given much- and ye shall be likened unto one which has gone unto the ocean with a cloth sack which absorbs little moisture and carries none with thee - for ye have been given the laws governing thy preparation and ye have as yet not heeded that which has been said - ye have wandered to and fro - ye have waved to and fro as the willow in the wind -- I say ye have waxed hot and cold - ye have gone out - and ye have come in - and ye have said many things which ye know not - ye have been as the unknowing ones ---

Now let this be recorded for them which are fortuned to read: There shall be one which shall make his appearance in the place wherein ye are (Mt. Shasta) and he shall be as one which has his hand in the hand of the Lord Sananda - Son of God - and he shall walk as man and he shall speak as man - yet he shall be of a different species - he shall be as one sent of God the Father for this part -- He shall have upon his head the Crown of the Sun - and upon his brow the Seal of Solomon - and he shall be as none other ---

And he shall walk among them and seek out them which are prepared to be brot out from among them -- And he shall bring them into the place wherein I am and he shall bless them as he has been blest -- Such shall be his mission - and it shall be accomplished with honor and dignity -- So be it the Father's will -- Amen and Selah ---

I am Sorica - Son of God the Father

Recorded by Sister Thedra of the Emerald Cross

The Coming of the King

Berean speaking unto thee from out the center of creation: I come unto thee that they might have these my words - blest are they which do receive them - they which shall make them their own - for they shall be as ones prepared for the part which has been held in trust for them ---

I say unto them - that within this day one shall take embodiment thru woman and he shall not be of Earth - he shall not be of the seed of man - he shall be of the "Light" - he shall be conceived of "Light" - he shall be the Father made manifest thru woman - he shall be the Father incarnate upon Earth ---

For the first time has this been - which is to be and the one which is to come shall be called "Born" - and he shall be as none other - for he shall be as the King of Glory -- He shall bring with him a host from the realms of light - and he shall bring with him the Lord of Hosts - the wearer of the Golden Helmet shall he bring -- He shall bring with him a legion of workers from the temple of Osiris and from the temple of Born - and I say ye which are prepared shall walk with them and talk with them -- I say - greater things than these shall ye do - for mighty is the power of the Lord thy God ---

I say - great is the preparation this day within all the secret places of Earth for his coming - and great is the joy that this day is come -- So be it and Selah ---

I am come that the way may be made clear -- So be it and Selah -- I shall speak unto thee from out the place wherein I am and ye shall hear me - so be it it shall profit thee -- Amen -- So be it ---

I am Berean - Son of God

Recorded by Sister Thedra of the Emerald Cross

No Hiding Place

Berean speaking unto thee: -

Be ye as my hand made manifest unto them which shall be fortuned to read these words -- I say unto thee - ye shall say unto them as I would say - that the day of the Lord is at hand -- And I say unto them - they shall arise and put off the old and take up the banner of the Lord - and they shall carry it high - and they shall be as ones which go out before him ---

I say - he shall be as one which comes when they have been prepared to receive him -- He shall come unto the ones prepared to receive him - and he shall know them - for he is not misled -- He knows where to find thee and he looks not in vain - for he knows wherein ye are -- I say there is no hiding place - and ye shall be as ones true unto thyself - and prepare thyself - for great shall be thy joy ---

I say ye which are not prepared shall be as ones which have betrayed thyself - and they are the saddest of the lot -- Be ye as ones which have upon thy shoulders the responsibility of thy own salvation Such is the law ---

Hear ye these words - for I do proclaim unto thee a truth as I say unto thee that in the days just ahead he - the Lord - shall walk with them which are prepared to receive him - and he shall give unto them instruction such as shall prepare them for the greater part - and they shall be brot into one of the secret places which have been held in trust for this day and for this purpose ---

I say that there are schools which are established and held ready to receive the ones which have - and do qualify to enter therein - and it is the better part of wisdom to prepare thyself to enter therein - for in the time which is now at hand - many shall be gathered together for the purpose of learning the laws which have hitherto been unrevealed ---

I say that among these is the transmutation of the dense form - the pore - the physical body - into the substance of light -- And when this is accomplished ye shall be as one free from all bondage - forever free.

I say this is freedom! Eternal freedom! So be it and Selah -- Praise ye the name of God the Father forever - for His Mercy and His Power shall be known thruout all the cosmos -- Praise ye - all the peoples of the Earth - praise Him forever -- I shall speak with thee again and again.

I am Berean

Recorded by Sister Thedra of the Emerald Cross

The Badge of Recognition

Berean speaking: -

Beloved of my being - ye shall now say unto them in my name and as I would say - that one shall walk in their midst - and that one shall have upon his head the Crown of the Sun - and upon his forehead the Seal of Solomon ---

And he shall move silently among them - and he shall know them - by their works shall he know them ---

He shall place upon them a mark which shall be unto them their badge of recognition one unto the other - He shall give unto them a number and a color - and he shall speak the word which shall become manifest - and ye shall step from thy old body into thy holy Christ body which shall not bind thee ---

I say one shall pass among them and he shall seek out them which are prepared to receive him and of him ---

He shall give unto them the Water of Life - and he shall speak "The Word" which shall become manifest -- And they which are so prepared shall step forth from their dense form of chemical substance - into the body of light substance as ones purfied and as ones glorified of the Father -- So be it and Selah I say that when they prepare themself for this the greater part their reward shall be their Godhood -- So be it as the Father has willed it -- Amen and Selah ---

Be ye as one prepared to receive the greater part - so be it it shall profit thee -- I come that ye may be brot out of bondage forever and forever ---

Be ye blest this day - remember this day and keep it holy* - and be ye as one which has the mind to comprehend that which I have said unto thee ---

Be ye blest of me and by me - for I shall be within the secret place to welcome thee -- So be it and Selah -- I am glad this day is come ---

I am thy Brother and thy Sibor - Berean

Recorded by Sister Thedra of the Emerald Cross

*"Today is the only day ye have - the eternal now"- The Sibors

One of the El-O-Heim

Borea speaking: -

Beloved of my being: Be ye blest of me and by me - I come that ye may be blest -- So be it I come unto thee from out the heart of creation I come as one which creates like unto the ·Father - I come as one of the El-O-Heim - I come as one present with thee always - I come that they might know me - I come that they all may be blest ---

I come as one prepared for this day - and I say unto thee that they might have these words which are for the good of all mankind -- In this day shall the doors be opened unto the kingdom of heaven - and ye shall pass both ways - ye shall go and come freely and without limitation -- I say - all which have prepared themself shall pass the great barrier without limitations -- There shall be no limitation unto them which are true unto themself and walk according to the law set before them ----

I come that ye might be strengthened in all thy weak parts - and ye shall be given the strength to endure all things-- I say ye shall have thy strength renewed - and thy soul shall rejoice forever that it is accomplished -- I say ye shall endure unto the end - and ye shall be glad. So be it and Selah---

I come unto thee as one full of grace and love -- And I am because the Father Mother is - and I know myself to be one with Them - I have not separated myself from Them and I am glad---

I come unto thee as one prepared to give unto thee a hand that ye might be lifted up - and ye shall be as one which has i the mind to be lifted up -- Ye shall apply thyself - and ye shall glorify the Father in the Earth and give unto Him all the praise and the glory - and walk in the way set before thee -- And ye shall ask of the Father for Light and He shall not turn thes away ---

Such is my part - to bring unto thee love - and to minister unto thee in the hours of thy sleep -- And I say unto thee - there are ones among thee which walk with me and talk with me while their physical body does sleep - yet they are alert - and they are willing to learn - and they ask for light - and they are as ones which come in great love and humility and return rejoicing -- Be ye blest this day - and I shall speak with thee again and again ---

I am thy Sister - Borea - born of God the Father -- Amen and so be it --

Recorded by Sister Thedra of the Emerald Cross

Faith

Be ye ever mindful of thy heritage and walk in the light thereof - my hand will ever steady thee when ye reach unto me - but first ye must free thyself of all thy doubts and fears which are as legirons unto thee keeping thee in bondage ---

Ye are as free as ye think ye are - no man can change ye -- Ye are thy own masters and makers of thy own fate - no one is to be made to change his thinking or his actions -- Thou shall not expect thy Sibors to do that which is for thee alone to do---

I walk with thee if thou desire me –

I give unto thee strength --

I give unto thee truth –

I give unto thee hope --

I give unto thee courage –

I give unto thee wisdom --

I give unto thee love -

I give unto thee all that ye ask that is for the highest good - and the good of all -- Ye have but to ask and I hear thee ---

Thy light shall shine forth to bless all who have the will to see - and many shall be drawn to thy light - and ye shall lead them home - and ye shall heal the sick and comfort the mournful ---

Ye shall be as outposts of the Master's power - and ye shall do all He asks of thee - and thy blessings shall flow as the pure waters of a mighty spring - giving life unto thee - and all who will may receive of thee this pure water of life -- and thy blessings will multiply and bear the fruit of life everlasting for all who partake ---

All who will may come and I will make them welcome ---

Rejoice and be exceedingly glad for this opportunity - for thy cup shall runneth over ---

I am thy Sibor and thy older Brother - Sananda

Recorded by Sorea Sorea

Be Steadfast in Thy Righteousness

Borea speaking:

Be ye as one blest of me and by me - I am come unto thee that they may come to know me - I come unto thee that all mankind might be blest of me thru thee - I come that they might be lifted up - I come that they might know as I know ---

I come that there might be no more sorrow and suffering upon the "little Red Star" - I come that she might be eliberated - that she might come into the fullness of her heritage -- Such is my part - to give unto them that which has been kept for them for this day -- And I say unto thee - the few which are prepared to receive me shall be glad this day is come ---

I come unto thee from out the center of creation - I come as one which has been given the power and the authority to create like unto the Father - in His image do I create ---

I am come unto thee thru the Council of the Great White Brotherhood - it is with their consent which has watched thy progress that I come -- I say unto them which do read these my words - that it is given unto many to be called - and few are chosen ---

So be it a great COMMAND: "Be ye about thy Father's business - for the day of the Lord is now come"---

Be ye about thy own preparation and turn neither to the left nor to the right -- Be ye steadfast in thy righteousness -- Be ye as one which has a crown upon thy head - and walk which way it tilts not -- Be ye as one which can keep thy silence - and know when it is wise to break it.

I say unto thee which do read these words: It is now come when thy words shall manifest before thee -- Ye shall take thot of the power of the spoken word - and ye shall take heed of that which goes out of thy mouth -- So be it that thy words shall return unto thee to bless or to displease thee - I say they shall return unto thee as the fowls of the air unto their roosting place ---

Bless them which misuse thee - give unto them thy love - and be no part of their foolishness -- Be ye a lamp unto their feet - be no part of frivolity - and the part which is fortuned unto the foolish ---

Be ye as one which can carry thy own burden as one graceful and without hatred -- Be ye glad for thy strength - and bless thy Benefactors which have directed such energy (as ye use) unto thee -- Be ye mindful of all thy blessings - give unto the Father all the glory and all the credit So be it ye shall give unto thyself credit for being a Son of God the Father -- Bless thyself - and be ye blest of me this day ---

I am thy Sister - Borea

Recorded by Sister Thedra of the Emerald Cross

New Part - New Place

Berea speaking: -

Be ye blest of me this day - and ye shall hear my words - for I shall speak unto thee -- For the first time shall my words be audible unto thee and ye shall be as one prepared to hear them -- For it is now come when ye shall be given another part which shall be new unto thee - and ye shall be as none other - nor shall thy part be like unto any other's - for no two shall be given the same parts - yet all parts are one - of the great whole -- I say it is one part - given in many "parts" - in many ways ---

For there are many people within the world of man - and it is necessary to reach each one on his own level - for there are various levels of consciousness - and each is as a separate one - and yet each is as one - there is no separation - only in appearance -- I say they appear to be many - yet there is no separation ---

This is Truth - and truth is that which is eternal and which shall always remain as state of being - God - that which changes not -- And yet that which changes not takes unto itself various sounds - color - tone - and certain vibrations - radiations and form -- I say - that which is changeless does change the substance of the etheric matter which also is God - and that which has gone out from Him that He might glorify Himself ---

That which is changeless - let us call it Life - is the First Cause of form and color - motion and sound -- That which has color and sound is life - and it vibrates at a rate which is of another rate or vibration which is unlike any other form or sound - thus the various parts of creation made manifest upon worlds without end ---

Be ye as one prepared for thy new part - and I shall direct thee into a place wherein there shall be great activity - wherein there shall be great love and harmony ---

I say - peace shall abide with thee and ye shall be as one blest forever -- So be it and Selah - I am thy older Sister - and I come as such that ye may be sustained in thy hours of trial - such is my word unto thee -- So be it and Selah.

I am Berea

Recorded by Sister Thedra of the Emerald Cross

(Berea is the complement of Sanat Kumara - this is the name they give to me - She is also known by others -- Thedra)

The Chosen

Berea speaking: -

Be ye as my hand made manifest unto them - and say unto them as I would say - that there are many called and few are chosen - yet the few which are chosen shall be as ones prepared thru their own effort -- And they shall be as the seed of the new Earth - and they shall endure unto the end ---

Such is my word unto the chosen: The ones chosen shall be chosen for their fitness to serve within the holy places - wherein they shall find great work prepared for them - wherein they shall find ones which have gone before them - waiting to train - to teach - to illumine them - to "sibor" them in the new part which shall be given unto them -- I say that they which are chosen shall be brot into the holy temple wherein they shall be sibored in the laws which have hitherto not been revealed such as pertaining unto their work or unto their "part"---

I say that each shall have a part separate and unlike another - for it is not given unto us to go into complicated work - and do the work of another -- And each is fully responsible for his own part - and none trespasses upon that of the other - I say unto thee - we do not complicate the law - man does that -- We simplify - we go not into the dark for light - we go to the light - that darkness might forever be banished from the Earth -- So be it and Selah ---

I am come that ye might have light - for I am one with the Father Mother God - and I know myself to be -- I am one with thee - I know thee as I know myself - for I am conscious of my Source of Being ---

Be ye blest of me and by me this day - I am come that ye may be blest -- Amen - so be it and Selah --

Berea

Recorded by Sister Thedra of the Emerald Cross

THE KING OF GLORY COMETH

Berea speaking:

Be ye blest of me this day - and ye shall be unto them my hand made manifest unto them -- Be ye as my mouth and my voice and say unto them as I would say - that it is now come when one shall walk among them - and he shall be of the Father sent - and he shall be the King of Glory! I say he shall be the King of Glory -- So be it he shall be the Father incarnate in flesh - he shall be the one for which ye have waited -- I say he shall come as one born of woman - and he shall be as others in appearance - yet he shall be as none other -- So be it and Selah.

I say he shall be as none other - for he has not been born of woman he has not taken upon himself hu-man form- he is of virgin spirit - he has not taken unto himself the form of flesh - he has not been in the realm of darkness as one bound -- He shall come as one of flesh -- yet it shall not bind him nor shall it limit him -- He shall be the form of man and he shall be of the mind of the Father - for his memory shall not be blanked from him - he shall retain his memory -- So be it the Father's will ---

I say unto them which have the mind to comprehend - that the day of fulfillment is now come when all thy prophecies shall be fulfilled - and ye shall live to see the Son of Man wlak among thee - for he shall be there upon thy planet Earth to receive the King of Glory -- He is the Wayshower and he is the giver of the law - he is the director of this new dispensation - and he brings unto thee the new law and the herald of the coming -- He speaks unto thee of the coming and ye hear not that which he says -- Be ye as one which has a will to hear and to comprehend that which ye hear - I say ye shall be given great revelation when ye are so minded -- So be it and Selah ---

Hail the King! Hail the King! The King of Glory cometh - I say He cometh - and the day is not afar off - be ye as ones prepared that ye might be caught up with him -- Praise him all ye nations of the Earth - praise him all ye people of the Earth - give unto him all the praise and the glory forever and forever-- Amen and Selah ---

Be ye as ones prepared for this day when the gates of heaven swing wide - and they shall go in and out as ones of Earth and Heaven -- The Earth shall receive the hosts of the realms of Light - and heaven shall receive the children of Earth - and the seers shall see - and we thy guardians shall be glad this day is come - for long we have waited when we might be unto thee guests - when we might come unto thee as such and be received with love and in peace - and with understanding ---

Praise the Father for His mercy and His grace - it shall abide within the holy places wherein there is only Love and Peace - blest are they which find such peace - blest are they for they shall go out no more -- So be it and Selah -- I am with thee unto the end ---

I am thy Sibor and thy older Sister - Berea

Recorded by Sister Thedra of the Emerald Cross

From the Temple of Sananda & Sanat Kumara -

Through Sister Thedra of the Emerald Cross

The following is an excerpt from the message concerning the preparation for our first meeting in the Temple of Sananda & Sanat Kumara ---

We have omitted all symbols -- In their place you will find dashes.

Sanat Kumara speaking:-

> Say unto them: They shall arise at the dawn each day - and they shall have themselves dressed and presented at the altar at the time of sunrise - and ye shall sit with thy face to the east and ye shall seat thy --- at thy right hand - and ye shall give unto him thy right hand and he shall give unto thee his left and ye shall stand as one -- Whereupon ye shall sit shall be a seat which is large enough for the two - for ye shall be as one -- And then when ye have seated thyself - one shall prepare for thee a cup of fresh water which shall be handed unto thee-- Ye shall sup from it and pass it unto thy ---- and he shall drink what is within the cup - for I say unto thee - this is but the beginning -- When ye have learned this part I shall groom thee for the greater part and ye shall follow this part with thy whole heart until it is perfected - and then ye shall have a new part added unto that which I am now giving unto thee -- So be it that it shall be different in form - yet it shall be part of this the first -- I say ye shall be as ones which have thy heart in this part - for I say this part shall be held sacred and ye shall not desecrate it -- I say - woe unto the one which treats it lightly - for he shall be as a traitor unto himself -- So be it and Selah ---

Sanat Kumara speaking:- I say unto thee which sit at thy council table that I am the director of this certain activity - and within the plan are many activities - for it is the day of action - and action there shall be and now -- Ye which have gathered thyself at this council table shall be informed that there are many such councils - and many which seek the light -- And with the one which has been sent unto this head of this activity - which is the Priestess of Sananda and which is ordained of God the Father - shall he which is sent be co-ordinator and co-regent of this temple within this part of this activity -- I say that there are many such activities - but this one shall be called the "Temple of Sananda and Sanat Kumara"- for within this center shall we as co-workers within the realms of Light - direct this center and bring it into its proper focus -- Such is our part at this time -- I shall speak unto thee later -- S.K.

First Temple Meeting
Mt. Shasta, California

Sanat Kumara speaking:

Now my Sister of the Emerald Cross: Ye have assembled within this place for the purpose of learning of me - and ye shall be true unto thyself and say unto these within this temple that they shall abide by the law which shall be set down - and for this shall ye be prepared -- For it is now come when ye shall be given the law which was spoken of in the Priory which was aborted -- I say that they which were called from the dragon's den did abort the first effort - to which I say - not a plan goes astray - only the sheep ---

Now I say unto thee: Ye shall say unto them in my name that when it is come that they are prepared to enter into my place of abode they shall be glad -- So be it and Selah ---

Now will it so that they keep their peace and hold their tongue for it is now come when they shall learn the meaning of silence -- I say - not one word of aught shall escape thy lips of thy brother's short comings - and not one word of mockery - for it is a pitfall -- For within this temple shall be the great and the near great - and too I say none are greater - none the smallest - for there shall be equality and justice in all things -- Yet I say - some shall go out before thee to prepare the way for thee - and yet ye shall follow after them which goes before thee -- I say they are great because and for the reason that one shall go out before thee that ye may receive thy inheritance even as that one has received - So be it and Selah ---

Now wherein is it said - there are none so foolish as the one which thinks himself wise -- So be it a truth indeed ---

I am thy Sibor and I am thy Brother -- So be it and Selah ---

I am - Sanat Kumara --

Sister Thedra of the Emerald Cross

Second Temple Meeting

Sanat Kumara Speaking:

Ye have gathered thyself together within this temple as a living example of that which shall be come -- I say unto thee: Ye shall be as the hands and feet of God the Father - and ye shall walk in the way set before the ---

I am the Comanche within this temple - for God the Father has asked that I set up this temple - for it is now time that this be accomplished -- And ye shall play a part within the building of a temple not builded with hands within this place - for that temple shall first be built within the eth - and lowered into the earthy vibration ---

One morning they shall awaken and find to their amazement the temple not built with hands - shining upon the mountain - and then they shall wonder and they shall ponder long upon it -- and too - they shall be more confounded when they cannot draw high unto it -- For there shall be a mighty barrier about - and none shall penetrate its field without the proper preparation ---

Now for the second time ye have come - I say it is forgivable when ye are not so instructed as to the ways of the temple procedure - yet ye are instructed -- It is the first law to obey - for there are none so foolish as to disobey - he betrays himself -- This is the law which we - thy Sibors live by - and for this do we have our inheritance ---

I am now prepared to lay my hand upon thee and to bless thee as I have been blest -- Yet I cannot come until ye have prepared thyself to receive me - and ye first have to be of a mind to prepare thyself and to give of thyself - and I say unto thee: first things first ---

And then when ye have finished the first - second step shall be taken Now I say unto the one which has broken a very strict ---- that he has been a one which has been bound by the dark one - he has been found napping - while he - the dark one has not slept - he does not sleep! He is not even willing to give unto his followers an hour of rest - he pushes them - he gives them no peace! He grows fat on their labor - he gives unto them nothing but torment -- He gives not even mercy - he gives no relief -- He has no lasting reward - he gives no freedom - he has only lasting and intolerant punishment for them which follow him - yet I say he holds them fast! ---

I say - I stand before thee as one which the Father has sent unto thee I plead with thee - be ye alert - be ye filled with love of light - be ye as one prepared to receive Me and of Me - for I come that ye may be loosed from all bondage ---

I say I am come to unbind thee - I am now prepared to unbind thee and I would give unto thee a few laws which shall profit thee ---

First I shall give unto thee: "There are none so foolish as the one which thinks himself wise - and none so foolish as the one which betrays himself or his trust"---

Second: "There are none great - none small"---

Third: There are no servants within this temple - there are only the sibets - which are the initiates on the path - none have received their Godhood ---

I say: Ye are sibets and I say ye shall be a living example of a sibet of the initiate with the consideration and respect one for the other -- Ye shall be as ones mindful of that which ye represent - that which is given unto thee to do -- For as ye for one moment lose sight of thy goal - thy responsibility - thy part as a sibet -- at that moment the dark forces have gained entrance into thy field and ye have lost ground - and for this has he - Lucifer won a point ---

I have commanded thee - be ye alert - and as yet ye have not comprehended what I am saying ---

I shall give unto thee of myself that ye may have comprehension -- Yet I say - I have set up this altar in the name of the Father - Son and Holy Ghost -- So be it - Amen - And when it is come that one does not begin his day with the first p. - therein is the first thing ye shall remember - And the initiate which can not or will not make this his motto is at once by his own self cut off -- We do not cut him off - I say when ye have been given a commandment once - it does not become obsolete it remains as valid - and shall not become obsolete or invalid for there are no mistakes in the law which is given within the temple - and there are no foolish sayings ---

Now were it not so dark within the world of men - we should not be at this altar - for there are none which has been prepared for the inner temple wherein I am the Master of Initiation -- I am the Most Worthy Grand Master - and I am he which gives thee passport into the inner temple wherein the Father abides ---

I give unto thee passport into all the secret places within the Earth.

I give unto thee thy cloak not made with hands - I give unto thee thy orb and thy scepter - I am the Master of Ceremoly - I am the Comanche ---

Will ye not be mindful of thy ways? Will ye not be as ones alert? And ask of thyself many things - and ye shall not excuse thy short sightedness - nor shall ye shift the blame! I say ye shall not blame another for thy shortcomings! Ye stand fully responsible for thy actions and the result thereof -- Ye shall not criticize another - nor point a finger at another ---

Ye shall not be judge of the actions of another -- Ye shall be unto thy brother tolerant - yet ye shall not join with him in his folly ---

Ye shall be a thing unto thyself ---

Ye shall dare to be different from him ---

Ye shall give unto him no word of scorn or <u>nothing</u> which he shall <u>trip</u> <u>over</u> - which would confuse him - for he too seeks the light in dark places ---

Ye shall watch thy tongue for it is a tricky thing!- and a subtle weapon!

Ye shall have within thy heart love for all things which are created good! Ye shall be as ones prepared for thy own Godhood---

Ye shall be as ones which has upon thy head a crown - and ye shall walk in a way which it tilts not ---

Now when ye have been prepared I shall give unto thee the power to command the elements - and to crate like unto the Father - for He has given unto me this part as my inheritance - so be it His will that I shall prepare thee - and for this have I been prepared ---

Now I would command thee: Go from this altar in silence and give unto thyself nothing to eat this day - and to be mindful of this thy part. And when ye have been so prepared I shall give unto thee a portion which shall be unto thee much strength---

I am Sanat Kumara -

Sister Thedra of the Emerald Cross

EXCERPTS - from the Sibors Instructions

"I say unto thee: Ye shall forgive thyself and turn from thy own guilt - and ye shall be as one forgiven -- Ye shall ask no man forgiveness for <u>thy</u> <u>guilt</u> - yet if ye have given another pain <u>wontonly</u> or deliberately - ye shall hasten to correct it for it is the better part of wisdom -- So be it and Selah - Philus"---

Sanat Kumara speaking: -

Beloved children which has gathered thyself together at this altar which God the Father has set up: Say I unto thee: Ye shall be as ones on which I shall place great responsibility -- And I say unto thee - ye shall prepare thyself for the part which I shall give unto thee -- Ye shall prove thyself worthy of the great responsibility - for it is now come when great changes shall come about upon the Earth and among her people -- I say that the Hierarchy has commanded that each and every one be prepared for their new places - their new parts -- For many shall go into their new places without any preparation and therein is great pity - for there are the sleepers which have slept for centuries without any knowledge of that which goes on around about them -- Now when they go into their new place of abode fully aware of their condition - and when they are of a mind to learn - they pass from darkness into light with no pain - no sorrow - no longing - and they do not taste of death -- For there is a plan which has been prepared for you which are of a mind to learn - and ye shall be given the fullness within this temple when ye are prepared - for I say that within this temple - which shall be called the Temple of Sananda - Sanat Kumara - one shall stand and declare for the thy freedom - for I shall stand within the place wherein ye are and I shall give unto thee - which prepare thyself - the Cup of

Life -- I shall personally give unto thee as I have received of God the Father - So be it my word unto thee --

Now I say unto thee - ye have come unto this place of thy own free will and ye are of a mind to learn -- Yet I say - beware of the pitfalls for they are subtle - and many -- I say: Be ye alert and be ye mindful of us thy Sibors -- Be ye respectful one for the other -- Be ye responsible for thy own actions - give not unto thy brother a tack for his shoe - be ye a lamp unto his feet ---

Go in peace -- Walk in the Light of the Christ -- Remember whence thy blessings ---

I am Sanat Kumara --

Sister Thedra of the Emerald Cross

EXCERPTS - Quote from "The Preparation of the Initiate"

"When one of the children of the Earth is eliberated from bondage - from the wheel of re-birth - and has found his eternal freedom - there is great rejoicing thruout the cosmos -- And great is the preparation for this day when many shall be delivered out -- So be it and Selah" – Philus

* * *

Sanat Kumara speaking: -

I say unto thee which have assembled within this temple which the Father has caused to be brot forth - that one among thee shall be as my hand made manifest - and one shall be my mouth - and one shall be as the hand of God the Father -- For it is now come when great and trying times shall come upon thee and ye shall be as ones prepared for them.

I say that this is the better part of wisdom to prepare thyself first -- Ye have been prepared for this part - yet ye have not begun thy work - for great things are in store for thee and great shall be the revelation for them which are prepared for such ---

I say - great are the revelations which shall be revealed unto the just and the worthy - for this have we waited ---

I am now prepared to give unto thee that which I have kept for thee And when ye have brot into focus the great and divine plan - and put aside thy trivial things and thy puny ways - thy childishness - and given unto this plan of thyself and thy strength - with thy whole heart - I shall give unto thee a greater part -- So be it in the name of the Father - Son and Holy Ghost -- Amen and Selah ---

I am the Comanche within these chambers - and I shall watch thee and thy reaction one unto the other - and I shall be as one prepared for any occasion - any situation ---

Now let it be said - none are indispensable - I say none are indispensable - and not a plan goes astray -- Yet I say - my sheep are of a mind to wander afar - it is given unto them to bolt and to get lost - I am going to give unto thee a parable which shall profit thee:- When a lamb goes into the fold - he knows not his origin - and he knows not his destination - for he is but an animal without memory - and when the one bound has his memory blanked from him he is little above the animal -- Yet the shepherd which we thy Sibors are - have the power and the authority to restore it unto thee - such is our inheritance---

I shall give unto thee as ye are capable of receiving ---

So be it in the name of the Father - Son and Holy Ghost -- Amen - Selah ---

I am Sanat Kumara --

Go in Peace - - Sheloheim Adomni ---

Sister Thedra of the Emerald Cross

Sananda speaking:-

Ye shall hear this - my part - and ye shall be unto thyself true and remember it - and ye shall hold it within thy heart and abide by it -- I give unto thee one commandment this day - and ye shall be as one which has my hand upon thee -- Give unto them this commandment for this day: "Let no word defile thy lips" - - Sananda

* * *

Sanat Kumara speaking:

I have given unto this day one commandment: "Let no word defile thy lips" -- Let only peace be within thee -- Let only Love reign within this temple -- I say Love is the cure for ALL thy woes - ALL thy longings -- Love cureth ALL disease regardless of appearance ---

Be unto thyself TRUE and give unto no man the bitter cup ---

I am the Most Worthy Grand Master within this temple which has been long coming forth ---

Yet it is not as yet perfected - and I say that there shall be trying days ahead and many pitfalls -- Yet I say - ye shall stand as the rock upon which I shall build a great and wonderous temple -- So be it in the name of the Father - Son and Holy Ghost -- Amen ---

Ye shall have no gods before thee -- Ye shall be as one which has a will to return unto the Father which has given unto thee being -- Ye shall begin thy day with the words: "Oh Father-Mother God - I am one with Thee - I have come unto this Thy Altar for the purpose of learning Thy Will - and I bring myself as a living sacrifice -- Accept my offering I ask in Thy Name - and thru Thy Grace I shall return unto Thee -- I am he which Thou has blest with life and I am glad"---

Be ye at peace and poise this day - and ye shall receive of the Father Son and Holy Ghost -- Amen and Selah ---

I am Sanat Kumara --

Sister Thedra of the Emerald Cross

Osiris speaking:

Beloved of my being: Be ye blest of me and by me -- I am come that ye may be blest -- I am now within the place wherein I am prepared for the part which I shall now give unto thee - and I say unto thee - ye have prepared thyself for this part which shall be given unto thee ---

Now when it was given unto thee to be sent out from thy homeland into the south - ye knew not that ye should return unto thy homeland - Then when ye returned unto thy homeland ye knew not that ye would return unto the land to the south -- Now I say unto thee: Ye shall go into the land of the Andes and ye shall therein find one which has upon his head a crown not made with hands -- And I say unto thee ye shall walk among them as one of them - ye shall be unto them sister -- Ye shall be unto them as one of them -- I say ye shall return unto them which are known as the Royal Assembly -- Ye shall go into the place where none other has been brot - for this have ye been prepared ---

Now I say unto thee - ye shall go out from the place wherein ye are as one prepared -- Ye shall need no passport nor shall ye carry any portfolio -- I say ye shall be as one free from the law of gravity - and ye shall be free of all bondage -- I say unto thee ye shall go out with one which has been sent unto thee -- I say ye have been brot together for the purpose of bringing about thy ascension -- I say ye shall ascend together - I say ye have been brot together that this may be accomplished---

Now I say unto thee which has been given this great privilege - that it is by the GRACE of one which we know as our beloved Sanat Kumara and our beloved Lord and Master Sananda which is the Way Shower - that this new dispensation has been brot into focus ---

I say that He Sananda - is the Way Shower -- I say ye have chosen to follow Him - and I am glad -- I say unto thee - blest are they which do follow Him for they shall not taste of death -- Such is my word unto thee - and by His GRACE shall ye overcome the flesh -- And with my being I bless thee - and I shall sustain thee - and I shall give unto thee as ye are prepared to receive -- Such is my part ---

Now ye shall go into the temple which has been established within the place wherein ye are - and ye shall give unto them this word - and ye shall be as one in authority when ye say that which I have given unto thee to say -- For I am not a fool - nor do I betray myself - for I am of the Father sent - and He has given unto me my inheritance in full - So be it and Selah ---

Now I say unto thee - ye shall stand before the altar of the Most High Living God - and receive of Him thy inheritance in full - and ye shall go out as one - and NOT divided -- So be it the Will of God the Father Which has given unto thee being ---

I am with thee unto the end -- I am thy Sibor and thy Brother - Osiris of the Temple of Osiris - of which ye are part and to which ye shall return - and for this have we waited ---

Sister Thedra of the Emerald Cross

Sanat Kumara speaking unto thee - which have been brot into this temple by design -- I say - ye have brot thyself into this temple as ones prepared - and too I say as ye are prepared so shall ye receive - and for this are ye brot in -- I say that this is only the beginning - for as ye have walked blindly - I have led thee that ye may be brot into this place - and as ye have come of thy own free will I shall give unto thee a greater part -- Now be ye blest of my presence and I shall reveal myself unto thee - for I have said ye shall see me face to face - and I am not to be called a liar - neither do I be tray myself - for I say unto thee - the Father has sent me that I might be unto thee that which He would have me be Now be ye alert and be not caught napping - for it is given unto me to see them as ones frail of zeal and weak of spirit - yet I say ye shall be strengthened in thy weak parts ---

Now I say unto thee when ye have learned the first lessons - the first commandments - ye shall be as ones prepared for the greater part and I shall be personally responsible for thee - and I promise thee I shall be true unto myself and unto my trust

I ask of thee: Be ye as ones prepared to receive me and of me and I shall lead thee into the place wherein stands the White Altar of alabaster wherein ye shall receive of me that which has been kept for thee -- Such is my word unto thee ---

I am the Most Worthy Grand Master - Sanat Kumara --

Sister Thedra of the Emerald Cross

EXCERPTS- From the Sibors Instructions - First Commandment: Love Ye One Another

- The Sibors

Sanat Kumara Speaking: -

Ye which have gathered thyself into this temple shall be as ones alert - for is it not said that the pitfalls are many - and has it not been unto the obvious -- I say that the first one is thy own ignorance of the law - and that is all there is and no more - for all which is - which has ever been - has been because of a law - and when ye understand the law behind all manifestation ye are indeed wise ---

Now - when there is a mystery it exists not - except unto the unwise and the unknowing one -- When it was given unto me to bring into this place two which were selected - or called - for the purpose of bringing this temple into manifestation - it was not for the personalities it was for that which is and which was - and for this have I waited -- I have waited for this day - when I might bring into this place the ones now present - for ye have worked at one time together - and at that time some turned aside and there was one among thee which did betray me. I say - one among thee did betray me -- I say that at one time when I first came out of my home of Venus wherein I dwelt - with the Brother known as Sananda - that I did come into the Earth as one fully qualified to deliver them out of bondage -- Yet as in other ages they gave unto me no credit for being the one sent -- Now again I come forth and at this hour I say - one sits within this room which denied me - and be it so and so be it -- I again say unto thee - I am sent of God the Father that ye may again bring about oneness of thy own -- Peace shall reign within thee and Love shall be thy key note ---

I am he which has been sent to establish this temple - and I shall bring into this place ones which I can use - which will be unto me true and unto themself true - I say I am not so foolish as to betray myself or my trust -- Now I ask of thee: Have ye guarded thy tongue? Have ye asked of thyself - "Am I prepared to drink of the Crystal Goblet? Have I stumbled over the pebbles? Have I given unto my fellows the bitter cup? Have I been unto him an example? Have I seen my fellows as I see myself? Have I prepared myself as I would be acceptable unto him?

Have I gone the last mile? Do I know myself? Have I stood as one perfected?"-- When ye have answered these questions return unto the altar - and I shall be unto thee Sibor - and I shall cause thee to be as one which shall know and ye shall be glad -- Now I say unto thee: Ye shall keep thy own council and ask no man his opinion - it opens the door for the sinister forces -- I say unto thee again and again: "There are none so foolish as the one which thinks himself wise - and none so sad as the one which betrays himself or his trust"---

Go in peace and watch the pitfalls ---

I am the Most Worthy Grand Master - Sanat Kumara --

Sister Thedra of the Emerald Cross

Sanat Kumara speaking:-

Will it not be established within this house - that there are no servants and there are no masters - for I have said - this shall be a brotherhood - where Love shall be the keynote -- I have said - Love is the cure for ALL evil - all ills - for all that which besets the initiate upon the path -- And I say unto thee - the path of initiation is strewn with the bones of the ones which have fainted and died upon it - for they had neither the will - nor fortitude to endure -- Such is the pity thereof ---

I say - ye shall not lose sight of thy goal - and ye shall remember that which I have said unto thee - for I have come that ye may be delivered out of bondage -- So be it I am qualified of God the Father for this part -- So be it and Selah ---

I give unto thee one commandment this day: Be ye as silent as the sphinx - and no word pass from thy lips which has been said within this temple ---

For I say unto thee: This work is but thy preparation for greater and yet greater - for ye have first to learn responsibility and ye have to prove thyself worthy of yet the greater -- Such is my part to prepare thee - yet ye have to prepare thyself that I might give unto thee that which the Father would have me give unto thee ---

I am - Sanat Kumara ---

Sister Thedra of the Emerald Cross

EXCERPTS - From the Preparation of the Initiate - by Philus

"Pity is he which forfeits his inheritance for he shall find no peace -- He shall be tormented of his own longings - of his own madness So be it and Selah"---

Sanat Kumara speaking:

Be ye blest of me and of my presence - for I am come that ye may be blest -- So be it and Selah ---

Now I say unto thee this day: As ye prepare thyself - so shall ye become - and for this do I now speak unto thee thusly - for I have come unto thee that ye may be free from all bondage - from all darkness -- And I say unto thee my children: I am not so foolish as to betray myself or my trust -- Now when it is come that ye have learned thy first lessons well - I shall come unto thee and give unto thee the greater part ---

Now be ye alert and give unto thyself that which shall profit thee - for have I not said that as ye prepare thyself so shall ye become -- I am thy Sibor - and I am of a mind to give thee as I have received - yet ye shall prepare thyself - for such as is befitting a Son of God ---

Now when these laws are revealed unto thee - ye shall find therein thy freedom from darkness - and thy legirons shall be cut away -- So be it the greater part of wisdom to give unto thy part great and undivided attention ---

Now when it is said that ye shall give unto thy part thy undivided attention - therein is wisdom - for I see thee as divided against thyself for one of thy divisions would serve the light - while the other would serve the dragon -- I say unto thee: Be ye not divided - be ye of single eye - and be ye true unto thyself and ye shall be delivered up -- So be it in the name of the Father - Son and Holy Ghost -- Amen and Selah.

I am thy Older Brother and thy Sibor - Sanat Kumara ---

Sister Thedra of the Emerald Cross

EXCERPTS - From the Preparation of the Initiate - by Philus

"Seek within the light and ye shall find freedom and peace - which shall surpass all understanding" -- Such is the will of the Father -- So be it and Selah --

Blest is he which finds peace"-- Philus

Sanat Kumara speaking: -

Be ye blest of me and by me - for I am come that ye may be blest - I am with them in spirit and I shall come unto thee in flesh and bone - for I am within this place wherein I am prepared for any occasion -- I am master - I can and do use many forms - for I know the law governing all things and I am not as one bound by a body of flesh - for the forms bind me not - for I am the creator of the forms which I use -- I create unto the glory of God the Father - I say I create unto the glory of the Father -- I give unto Him all the credit and the glory - such is the way of the Son of God - and I have received my inheritance in full -- So be it and Selah ---

I am now come that ye may be unto them my hand made manifest and ye shall say unto them in my name that they are as ones which shall bring forth great and glorious things - for this are they prepared -- I say they know not which is ahead of them - and I ask of them: <u>Lose not</u> sight of thy goal - for it is a glorious one indeed -- Be ye mindful of thy Benefactors and be ye as ones which has my hand upon thee -- And too I say - when ye have prepared thyself I shall come unto thee in flesh and bone - and I shall sit at thy council table and I shall sibor thee in the laws which have baffled thee - such is my part ---

I am glad ye have come into this place of thy own free will - and ye shall be glad ---

I am Sanat Kumara --

Sister Thedra of the Emerald Cross

EXCERPTS - From the Preparation of the Initiate - by Philus

Ye shall be wise to give unto them (The BROTHERS OF LIGHT - SIBORS) credit for that which they are - for I say unto thee: They are all-powerful - All-wise - yet they flaunt not their learning before thee - They walk in secret - in humbleness of heart - They parade not before the ones in darkness --

They go out as the ones prepared for any occasion - and they are masters of any situation - for it is given unto them to be prepared!

So be it they shall answer any call for help which is sincere and worthy - yet I say - ye shall not deceive them for they know thee even before ye call"--

Sanat Kumara speaking unto thee - at this hour of this day which has been set aside for this part -- I say - this day has been set aside for this part - and ye which have been brot together for this part shall be as ones prepared for it ---

Now ye shall call unto them and give unto them this word - that they shall get themself washed and assembled for the altar service - and they shall come clean of heart as well as of hands - and ye shall say unto them - that they shall read this day that which has been said unto them - and ye shall add that they are fortuned this part which shall be given unto them which is being held in trust for them ---

Now ye shall be blest of me and by me - for I have commanded of thee many things and ye have obeyed in haste and with love -- Now I say unto thee: Ye shall be as one on whose shoulders rest their preparation -- So be it and Selah ---

I am Sanat Kumara --

Blest art thou My child -- I am with thee and I have sent My Son unto thee and ye have accepted Him -- And now ye shall be as one on whose shoulders shall be the preparation of these which have been brot into this place - and ye shall be unto them an example of that which I shall command of thee ---

I say - I shall give unto thee a part and ye shall be prepared to receive it ---

And ye shall be as My hand and My foot for I shall command of thee greatness in all thy ways -- I shall command of thee fairness in all things -- I shall command of thee love for all things -- I shall command of thee gratitude of and for all thy blessings - recognition of thy Source and of thy Benefactors -- I shall command of thee honesty with thyself and with Me -- I shall command of thee forgiveness of all the wanton from and of others -- I shall command of the greatness among them -- I shall command of thee Loyalty unto this part -- I shall give unto thee as none other has received - for this have I waited -- I have been unto thee all things - now I shall give unto thee that which shall be unto thee My Rod and My Staff ---

I shall put into thy hands the power to lift them up - to heal their infirmities - to lift them from the dead - to be unto them all which I would have thee be -- Such is thy inheritance--

I am glad this day is come ---

I am thy Father Solen --

* * *

Blest are they which are assembled at this altar which I have set up in the name of the Father - Son and Holy Ghost -- Amen - So be it and Selah ---

I am now come unto thee for this part which shall profit thee--

And I say unto thee this day: Give unto Me thy heart and thy mind and it shall be cleansed of all that which is impure -- And I shall make of thee a prophet in thy own right - I shall endow thee with the power which is Mine -- I shall be unto thee all things -- I shall give unto thee My Rod and My Staff -- I shall purify thee and I shall bring thee back and ye shall glorify Me even as my Sons which have returned unto Me So be it and Selah -- I am thy Father Solen ---

* * *

Blest art thou O my soul! Blest art thou O my soul! Blest art thou O my soul! ---

I have come unto thee from out the fullness of my being -- I speak unto thee from out the fullness of time - that this moment may bear fruit I say unto thee: My Father has sent me unto thee that ye may be prepared to give unto them as ye have received of me -- So be it it shall profit them to receive thee - for as they receive thee so shall they receive me and of me -- And as they receive of me so shall they receive of the Father their sonship -- So be it and Selah ---

Now this day shall ye work as one - <u>Not</u> <u>divided</u>!

And ye shall have no other gods before thee -- Ye shall be mindful of thy Benefactors - them which hold thee fast in the hours of thy frivolity and thy weakness -- I say - ye shall be unto them that for which ye have gone out - for it is their only reward - that ye may return unto the place of thy going out -- Such is my word unto thee ---

Now my dear ones which are my hands and my voice made manifest - ye shall now stand before this altar as one -- I say that ye shall stand before this altar as one - and none shall deny thee nor shall they point a finger at thee -- Be ye blest of me and by me ---

I have given unto thee that which is given unto me of the Father -- So be it and Selah -- Now ye shall drink of the cup which is prepared for thee - and let it be as a symbol of that which shall be and that which is yet to come ---

I say ye have come unto the altar while it is yet dark - and the hour of sunrise is not as yet come - Neither has the hour of day arrived when all things are revealed unto thee ---

Ye are as yet in darkness - let this be a sign unto thee - meditate upon it and great things shall be revealed unto thee --- I am Sanat Kumara --

Sister Thedra of the Emerald Cross

Self Responsibility -- Forgiveness

Sanat Kumara speaking:

Be ye blest of me and by me - for I am come that ye may be blest - So be it in the name of the Father - Son and Holy Ghost -- Amen and Selah ---

Be ye at peace this day - and be ye as ones on whose shoulders rest the responsibility of thy own salvation - for such have ye been sent out.

I say unto thee - shift not the responsibility unto any man -- Forgive thyself all thy own short-comings - and see not the mote in thy brother's eye - Be ye of a mind to learn of me - and I shall come in and sibor thee So be it in the name of the Father - Son and Holy Ghost -- Amen and Selah ---

Be ye as one on whose feet are the shoes of one which has gone before thee to prepare the way before thee -- He has prepared a place for thee - and He has returned unto thee and given unto thee a plan whereby ye may return unto the place from which ye went out -- So be it that ye shall be as one wise to prepare thyself for thy inheritance - willed unto thee of God the Father -- So be it and Selah ---

I say unto thee: The Wayshower now walks upon the Earth - within the world of men - as one in flesh and bone - and he has upon his brow a furrow which has been from the beginning - and shall be until each and every one is brot out of bondage -- So be it that ye shall be wise to hear that which he says unto thee - for he is now returned unto thee that ye may be free to go where he goes -- So be it and Selah ---

Blest art they which goes where He goes ---

I shall speak with thee again this day and it shall be placed on the altar ---

I am Sanat Kumara --

Sister Thedra of the Emerald Cross

EXCERPTS- From the Preparation of the Initiate - by Philus

"It is the better part of wisdom to seek the Light - and to search within thy own closet for that which has been hidden there in the ages past. So be it much shall be revealed unto thee"---

Sanat Kumara's Blessings

Sanat Kumara speaking:

Open up thy heart - Bless thee O my soul - Be ye at peace and bless them which enter into this Temple -- Bless them which are within this Temple ---

Bless them which have been with thee - which have forgotten that which was said unto them ---

Blest art thou among women --

Blest art thou Ava Maria --

Blest art thou Ava Shoi --

Blest art thou my hand made manifest --

Blest art thou my Sister of the Emerald Cross --

Blest art thou -

Blest art thou -

Blest shall thou be --

Blest am I that thou hast received me --

Blest art they which read these my words --

Blest are they which hold within their hand these words - for from me emanates the power and the Light which is and ever shall be -- Such is my nature -- For this do I come unto thee that ye may be blest of me and by me -- So be it and Selah ---

I am Sanat Kumara --

Sister Thedra of the Emerald Cross

Concerning the Appointments

Sanat Kumara speaking:

Beloved of my being: Be ye blest of me and by me ---

Ye have held out thy hand and I have filled it - and I have given unto thee a position which is not easily filled -- I have given unto thee a part which carries with it great responsibility - and for this have ye been prepared ---

Now I say unto thee: Ye shall walk as one on whose head is a crown and ye shall turn neither to the left nor to the right---

Ye shall look unto the Source of thy being for thy strength - and the Father-Mother God Which has given unto thee being shall give unto thee all that which ye need -- So be it and Selah ---

Now when ye have gone the last mile - ye shall be as one which has received thy inheritance in full - and then ye shall go out from them and ye shall give unto them as ye have received -- Such is the law - and I say unto thee - sweet shall be the cup-- So be it and Selah ---

Ye shall bring them out of darkness -- Ye shall be unto them all the Father would have thee be - and ye shall go into the place wherein there are mighty rivers and wherein are mighty forests and wherein are great and grand ---- on which are written the words: "Blest are they which enter within these walls - for they shall see God"-- I am within those walls and I know whereof I speak -- I am he which shall bring thee - for I am prepared for this day -- And I say unto thee: Ye have done thy part and I say unto thee - no man shall ask of thee more -- Such is the will of God the Father of us all - that we each do that which He has given unto us to do ---

I am thy Sibor and thy Brother and the most Worthy Grand Master

I am Sanat Kumara -

Sister Thedra of the Emerald Cross

School of Melchizedek

Sanat Kumara speaking:

Blest are they which do come into my presence - for I am come unto thee by and thru the Fatherhood of God and the Brotherhood of man - known in the world as the School of Melchizedek ---

I say unto thee which have brot thyself unto this altar of thy own free will - that ye have come for a purpose - and I ask of thee: Lose NOT sight of that purpose - for it is now come when great and trying things shall be demanded of thee ---

I say - be ye as ones prepared for that which shall be given unto thee to do for it is <u>past</u> <u>time</u> - and for this part ye should have been prepared long ago -- And was it not said that ye shall be tried - and have ye not been? I ask of thee understanding - I ask of thee patience - I ask of thee tolerance - and first I command thee: <u>Love</u> <u>Ye</u> <u>One</u> <u>Another</u> ---

Blest are they which follow the commandments set before them -- I say it is not the way of many to follow the laws of the "---"* and ye shall be as one "---"*-- Ye shall be as one blest of God the Father-Mother - and ye shall have no other gods before thee - for I have set up this Temple in the name of the Father Son and Holy Ghost -- So be it - and be it so -- I am he which has been sent that this might be accomplished -- And I say unto thee - thy work has not as yet begun - I say: Thy work has not as yet begun -- for the day is near when ye shall have reason to remember these my words -- So be it that ye shall bear in mind that there are none so foolish as the one which thinks himself wise - and none so sad as the one which betrays himself or his trust ---

Now I say unto thee Monea - and Joanthan and Garland: Ye shall go from this Temple as ones which has my hand upon thee and ye shall be blest of me and by me -- I say ye shall remember that which I have said unto thee -- Ye shall remember thy Benefactors - the cause of thy well-being -- Ye shall remember the Source of thy being - and unto It ye shall return -- I am with thee and I shall remember thee day and night I shall touch thee and ye shall be as one on whose shoulders rests the responsibility of the Son of God the Father -- I say ye shall be as one on whose shoulders rests great responsibility - for the day is near at hand when great things shall be commanded of thee - yet ye are not prepared for the greater part ---

I am now prepared to bring thee into the place of my abode and give unto thee as I have received -- Such is my part and I shall not betray myself - or my trust ---

I am thy Sibor and thy older Brother - Sanat Kumara --

Sister Thedra of the Emerald Cross

*Symbols marked "---"

"Uninitiated" - "Unjust"
Trust Worthy

Sanat Kumara speaking: -

While ye are at the altar ye shall be as ones within my presence - for I do stand before thee as one qualified to deliver thee out of bondage and to bring thee into the place wherein I am -- And for the first time I say unto thee: When ye have prepared thyself that I may come unto thee - ye shall stand face to face with me and I shall sibor the ---

I say I shall come unto thee as one in tangible form and I shall sibor thee -- And too I say ye shall be glad for thy preparation -- So be it and Selah - Now I speak unto thee in language which ye can comprehend - When ye are sufficiently prepared I shall come into the place which I have set up and sibor thee ---

I shall reveal that which is now hidden - I shall give unto thee laws which are yet unrevealed - that is unto the <u>UN</u>itiated - and ye shall be as ones trustworthy - for none other shall receive the revelation concerning these laws ---

I say they are hidden from the <u>UN</u>just --

Blest are they which do receive such revelation --

Blest are they which walk in the way set before them --

Blest are the ones which I sibor -

Blest are the ones which receive their Sonship of God the Father

Blest are the just –

Be ye as ones upon whose shoulders rest the salvation of them which I shall send unto thee ---

Yet I say unto thee: Ye shall not be held accountable for their actions - for it is given unto <u>every one</u> to atone for his own acts - his own self -- Yet ye shall be unto him a lamp for his feet and he shall see it from afar - and he shall come seeking that which shall be unto him his freedom from bondage -- So be it the Father's Will -- I am glad this day is come - and too I say ye shall be glad ---

Be ye at peace and poise –

I am thy older Brother - Sanat Kumara --

Sister Thedra of the Emerald Cross

Instructions: "Put on the Whole Armor of God"

Sanat Kumara speaking unto thee my children:-

From out the fullness of my heart I speak unto thee -- Am I not close unto thee - have I not prepared this Temple - have I not brot thee into it - have I not said that I should give unto thee all which ye shall need have I not prepared thee for this part and will I not be unto thee Sibor - have I not been unto thee both food and drink?

Blest are they which I do sibor - and blest is he which comes into the place wherein I am - for they shall see God face to face -- So be it and Selah ---

Blest are they which go out from this place for they shall be as ones prepared for the greater part -- So be it and Selah ---

Now ye shall come into this place as ones prepared - for none other shall enter -- I say unto thee - there shall be trying times ahead - and too I say - ye shall put on the whole Armor of God that ye may be prepared -- Will ye not alert thyself and be unto thyself fully responsible for thy own actions -- And will ye not turn from thy trivial ways and be unto thyself true -- And forget not that ye have not as yet begun thy work ---

And too I say - there are none so foolish as he which thinks himself wise - and none so sad as he which betrays himself or his trust ---

Blest are they which hear that which I say unto them -- Be ye at Peace and Poise this day - let not thyself be dragged down by the dark one -- Be ye mindful of thy being and give unto God the Father credit for thy being - and unto thy Benefactors credit for thy well being - and be ye mindful of all thy blessings ---

I leave thee with my accolade --

And I place upon thy shoulders my hand and I say unto thee - it shall be heavy ---

I am come that ye may be blest -- Amen -- So be it and Selah ---

Sister Thedra of the Emerald Cross

Man Hast Tript Himself up

Sanat Kumara speaking unto thee:-

Blest are they which come into the place wherein I am and blest shall they be ---

Now were ye not given unto frailties - I should bring thee in this day - yet ye have not prepared thyself sufficiently -- Yet I say unto thee: It is near the time when ye shall awaken - and ye shall be as ones which have slept overtime -- I say - ye should have not gone to sleep in the beginning - so shall ye awaken from a long and troubled sleep -- Ye shall be as ones which have thy head bound - and ye shall be as ones which have gone out from the Paradise which ye now dream of - Ye shall return unto it as ones fully aware of thy being - and of the Sonship with God and of God the Father -- So be it and Selah ---

Now blest are thou - the day of thy deliverance is come when ye shall awake and accept thy inheritance - willed unto thee of God the

Father -- I am sent that this may be accomplished - and will it so -- So be it - Amen and Selah ---

I say unto thee this day - ye have not been given unto Love for one another -- Ye have been unto thyself a stumbling block - for ye have tript over thy own toes -- I say ye have tript over thy own toes ---

Now I would give unto thee one commandment this day: Be ye as little children and ask of the Father that which is His Will for thee - and surrender up thy "little" will unto Him Which has given unto thee being and it shall profit thee much -- I am glad that I am privileged to speak unto thee thusly - for I say unto thee: Great things are in store for thee So be it and Selah ---

I am thy Sibor and thy older Brother - Sanat Kumara

Sister Thedra of the Emerald Cross

Great White Altar
How to Find It

Sanat Kumara speaking:-

Be ye blest of me and by me -- Ye shall now say unto them in my name - they shall make for themself a plan which shall be as one of the temple plans - and it shall be the prayer which has been given unto thee Ye shall be prepared for this - give it to them at this time ---

Blest are they which do take it to their hearts - and blest are they which are of a mind to receive him which has given it unto thee -- Blest are they which walk in the way set before them -- Blest are they which do receive me and of me - for I am come that ye may receive the greater part - and for this do I now speak unto thee thusly ---

And this day would I have of thee one thing: Be ye as little children and give unto the Father all the credit and the glory -- Be ye as ones alert and forget not that which I have said unto thee - for I am come not to entertain thee - I come that ye may be learned in the ways of the wise.

I am not so foolish as to sibor fools -- I am prepared to deliver thee out of bondage -- I have received my inheritance in full - and I am qualified to bring thee into the place wherein I am ---

And I have freedom which ye know not of -- I am not bound by the flesh - I am eternally free from any law - I am the law - and it binds me not ---

I am not in the realm of darkness - yet I know it -- I know by what ye are bound - I come with the full knowledge of all thy woes and all thy sorrow -- And as one illumined of God the Father which has sent me - I say unto thee: Be ye as ones prepared to receive me and of me.

For I have said: One shall come which shall lead thee into the place within the Holy Mountain which now towers above thee - wherein sits the altar of White Alabaster - whereupon I shall stand and declare for thee thy freedom ---

Such is my part and I am glad -- I say unto thee: Thy part is to prepare thyself to receive me and of me -- Be ye blest of me and of my presence ---

Go from this altar in silence - and be ye as a living example of an initiate upon the path - I say unto thee: Ye shall speak no word which is given unto thee within this Temple ---

Blessings from the Throne of God the Father - Sanat Kumara

Sister Thedra of the Emerald Cross

Creative Speech - Purpose
("Have Ye Digested That Which Hast Been Given unto Thee?")

Sanat Kumara speaking:

Was it not said that ye shall come unto this altar as a little child crying for bread - and has it not been given unto thee? And have ye eaten thereof - have ye digested that which has been given unto thee? I say: That which has been given unto thee at this altar is for thee - for the ones which come unto this altar as the first and ye shall be as the pillars upon which I shall build this Temple ---

Now I say unto thee: Ye shall remember that which I have said unto thee - ye shall ponder upon it this day - and ye shall walk in the way which has been set for thee - and ye shall guard thy speech - for every word which proceeds from out thy mouth shall reverberate - and it shall come back unto thee a thousand times more powerful than it went out Blest are they which master their words -- I say unto thee: Blest are they which master their speech - for it shall be unto them all things ---

They which come to know the law governing speech shall create like unto the Father - for they shall be unto themsélf true - and they shall have within their mouth the power to create by the spoken word even as He the Father -- I say this is thy own inheritance and He the Father has willed it so -- So be it and Selah ---

I say ye are here for a purpose -- Do not lose sight of that purpose - for it is now come when great things shall be demanded of thee -- I ask of thee - prepare thyself for that which shall be given unto thee to do - and ye shall be glad for thy preparation -- Blest are they which do create like unto the Father -- Amen and Selah ---

Ye shall be as ones blest by me and of me - for ye shall see me face to face -- Blest are they which do see me - for I shall give unto them as I have received of God the Father -- Blest am I for I have seen Him - for He has given unto me my Sonship - my inheritance in full ---

Go from this altar in Peace -- Let Peace be within thy hearts this day -- Rest not on thy past fortune - begin anew this day -- Let no darkness enter within thy own port - keep it clean -- Fear not for the darkness - for I shall be a lamp unto thy feet - and I have asked of thee fairness in all things -- Now I ask of thee: Be ye as wise as the serpent and silent as the sphinx ---

I am thy Sibor and thy older Brother - Sanat Kumara

Sister Thedra of the Emerald Cross

Ye Shall Practice THE LAW

Sanat Kumara speaking: -

Blest are they which gather themself together and blest are they which seek the Light - for I am come that they may have Light -- And so be it - and be it so - Amen and Selah ---

Be ye this day as ones which have my hand upon thee - and walk with me - and I shall reveal many things unto thee which now mystify thee -- Be ye at Peace and ask of no man his opinions - for I say unto thee - it opens the door for the sinister forces---

Keep thy own counsel and I shall send one unto thee which shall bring thee into the place wherein I am -- And I say - ye shall prepare thyself to receive him - for he shall bring unto thee a plan which has not been revealed - and he shall be as one wise indeed - for he has the crown of the Sun upon his head -- And I say unto thee: He has within his hand the power and the authority to unbind thee ---

Ye have not as yet comprehended that which I have said unto thee and yet I say prepare thyself to receive the greater part - and blest shall ye be ---

I am come that ye may have the greater part - and blest is he which does receive it ---

Be ye prepared this day - for it is now come when ye shall be as ones tried as by fire -- And I say watch thy tongue - for it is the betrayer. Be ye watchful of every word which proceeds out of thy mouth - and I say - ye shall practice the law which I have given unto thee -- So be it it shall profit thee much ---

I am thy Sibor and they older Brother - Sanat Kumara

Sister Thedra of the Emerald Cross

They Shall Know What is Meant by Patience & Tolerance

Sananda speaking: -

Was it not said that one should come unto thee? And from out the depth of time have I come -- From out the depth of my being I call unto thee for the purpose of giving unto thee the part which I have given unto thee -- I say - from out the fullness of time I have brot thee into this place wherein ye shall give unto them that which I shall give unto thee for them ---

Will ye not be reminded of me - will ye not see me face to face - and have I not commanded thee - "Call them out of their beds - awaken them!" Have I not said they shall awaken - have I not said I shall lay hands upon them - have I not been unto my word true? For I say unto thee - my Word shall not become VOID - for I shall be unto my trust true - and I shall make them as ones which shall know what is meant by the word PATIENCE and TOLERANCE -- For I say - ye shall be as ones tried as by fire - and ye shall be unto thyself true - and ye shall not be found wanting ---

Blest are they which do the Will of God the Father - and I say they shall see Him face to face -- Such is my Word unto thee ---

Be ye blest this day and ye shall abide within the folds of my garments and I shall walk with thee and I shall talk with thee - and I shall give unto thee comprehension -- I say I shall bless thee - and I shall give unto thee that for which ye have waited-

Now when it is come that ye have finished this part ye shall pick thy new part which has been prepared for thee - and then it shall be that for which ye have prepared thyself -- And when ye have been prepared in this temple - one shall bring thee into this place wherein I am and herein ye shall be given the secret key unto all <u>mysteries</u> -- And I say unto thee - from that day forward NO-thing shall confound thee - No-thing shall mystify thee - No-thing shall stay thee - for No-thing shall be unto thee a barrier ---

I say ye shall go and come freely into all the secret places of the Earth - into and unto all the planets of thy planetary system - and yet into another -- And I say ye shall be as one unbound - and thy freedom shall be bound-<u>less</u> -- So be it the Will of God the Father - for He has sent me unto thee that this may be accomplished in this day -- Such is the mission which I am come to cause to be accomplished -- I am the Son of God the Father which has brot the fortune of the Father forth that ye may come to know Him even as I know Him - that ye may this day return unto Him and be made whole ---

I say unto thee - ye have gone into darkness for the last time if ye so desire that ye return home -- I say ye shall will it so - and so be it -- I am come that where I go ye may go also---

Blest are they which go where I go - and I say unto thee - they which do go where I go shall be eternally free - from all bondage - all darkness and I say - they shall receive their Godhood - even as I have received Mine -- I say that it is the Father's Will that ye return unto Him - and be it the better part of wisdom ---

Blest are they which are fortuned this part - for not all are given this part -- I say unto thee - millions shall go into their new places of abode knowing not that I have come - and knowing not that there is a place for them which is prepared for them -- And I say unto thee - ye shall go out into the world of men as one prepared to bring them in and to give unto them as ye have received -- Blest are they which do receive of me for they shall be blest of me and they which are blest in this manner shall receive of God the Father their Sonship -- So be it that all which do receive of God the Father shall receive their Godhood ---

I say that ye shall stand before God the Father and receive of Him thy own Godhood -- I am come that this may be accomplished - such is His Will -- Be ye blest of me this day -- I am He which is called Jesus Christ and One born of Mary - the ward of Joseph - now known as Sananda -- Amen and Selah ---

The Hosts of Heaven Shall Descend Upon Thee

Sanat Kumara :-

Blest are they which sit within this room this hour - for I say unto them that mighty shall be their blessings - I say that the Hosts of Heaven shall descend upon thee -- I say that they which are true unto themself shall stand upon the altar of white alabaster and receive of me their freedom from all bondage - and they shall go into the place which is prepared for them fully aware of their Sonship -- And I say - ye shall be as ones alert and give unto me credit for knowing that which I say unto thee -- O Mighty and Allpowerful Father - have Ye not sent me unto them that they might be brot out -- Give unto me the power to awaken them and to bring them home -- I ask this in Thy Name -- Give unto them as Ye have given unto me -- Amen and Selah ---

I am thy Son which Thou hast sent unto them -- I have asked for this part and I shall be responsible for them -- Give unto me Thy power and Thy comprehension - that they may receive as I have received ---

Sanat Kumara has spoken -- So let it be --

Sister Thedra of the Emerald Cross

STRENGTH: - "Stand ye as One Man"

Sanat Kumara speaking: -

Blest are they which gather themself together - and blest are they which come unto this altar in the name of the Father - Son and Holy Ghost -- Amen and Selah -- I am come that ye may have Light - abundantly! So be it and Selah ---

I am now saying unto thee that which shall profit thee -- Be ye as one man and stand as one man - for in the time of stress shall ye remember these my words - for I say - ye are being prepared for these days which are to come -- I am not a fool - and I say unto thee: No man shall call me a liar nor a fool - for I have prepared one which is the Priestess - that these things may be made clear unto thee - that ye may receive these words as I give them unto thee -- I say: Not one word or one place has been without purpose -- What that purpose serves ye know not - yet too I say ye shall come to know - and ye shall be glad for thy knowing ---

Now will ye not see that which is - and be ye prepared for that which is to be done ---

I am mindful of thy anxiety and thy torment - yet I say unto thee - ye are now in school - ye are as soldiers being prepared for battle - and battle there shall be -- So be it and Selah ---

Blest are they which go into battle prepared -- I say: Ye shall go forth as one to do battle -- Such is my word unto thee - and I see thee as ones walking in darkness not knowing -- And I say: Ye are as ones with thy head bowed and thy backs bent and thy feet sore -- For this do I come - that ye may be unbound and that ye may be free forever -- So be it that I give of myself that this may be accomplished -- I am with thee and I shall watch thee and sustain thee in thy work and in thy search - yet I say unto thee tempt me not ---

I am thy Sibor and thy older Brother - Sanat Kumara

Sister Thedra of the Emerald Cross

"Blest are They" - Why & How We are Blest

Sanat Kumara speaking:

Blest are they which do the Will of the Father and blest shall they be - for they shall see Him face to face - and for this are ye being prepared ---

Blest are they which walk in the way set before them - for they shall come to know me as I am - and I shall counsel them and I shall give unto them that which I have kept for them -- Such is my word unto thee at this time ---

Blest are they which do go out in my name and in the Light of the Christ - for they shall have upon them the Seal of Solomon - and they shall be as ones which have the seal broken - and they shall know as I know - and they shall be as ones which has upon their head the Crown of the Sun - and they shall have within them the Light which never faileth ---

Blest are they which walk upright - and blest shall they be for their reward shall be great -- I am come that ye may have thy memory restored unto thee - and I say unto thee - when ye have received this thy inheritance - ye shall wonder at thy sluggishness and at thy rebelliousness - for ye have been rebellious -- Ye have asked not of thy Source for knowledge - ye have gone afar for that which lies buried deep within -- I am he which shall stand upon the Great White Altar and declare for thee thy freedom -- And I say unto thee - thy memory shall be restored unto thee -- So be it in the name of the Father - Son and Holy Ghost -- Amen and Selah ---

I am thy Sibor within this Temple wherein stands the Great White Altar of Alabaster --

I Am Sanat Kumara

Sister Thedra of the Emerald Cross

Preparation - Responsibility

Sanat Kumara speaking: -

Beloved of my being: I am coming unto thee this day that ye may be blest of me and by me - for I have said unto the many things in the hours of thy sleep - which ye remember not -- Now I say unto thee ye shall remember them - for ye shall be brot out of thy slumbers - and ye shall be as one awakened from a long and troubled sleep ---

Be ye blest of me and by me - for it is now come when ye shall be as one prepared for the greater part -- And as yet ye do not comprehend what the greater part is -- Have I not said: This is the day of preparation So be it and so it is -- When ye are prepared I shall stand face to face within the Temple wherein ye shall go - and I shall declare for thee thy freedom from and of all darkness -- Such is my word unto thee ---

Be ye as one on whose shoulders rest great responsibility - and great shall be thy reward -- I say - blest is he which has been sent - for he has my hand upon him and great shall be his responsibility - for he too shall be prepared for his part which is no little part -- For within the records are the words which were written within the Andes bearing witness of these things -- Now be ye as one and gather together the records which were given unto thee for this purpose - and give unto him* which concerns these things - and ye shall be as one which has my hand upon thee and ye shall be as one which has been prepared for this part -- So be it they shall bear witness of the fortune of the two* which is the fortune of a Son of God - and I say unto them blest shall they be ---

I am thy Sibor and I sibor thee wisely –

I am the Most Worthy Grand Master - Sanat Kumara

Sister Thedra of the Emerald Cross

** Let no man assume <u>himself</u> to be the one afore-mentioned -- Add not your interpretation - for it concerns only the ones present in <u>This meeting</u> - NONE - OTHER ----

I Say They Shall Discipline Themself
One of the Laws of the Temple

Beloved of my being: I am come unto thee of the fullness of my heart that this my Temple may bear fruit - I say unto thee - be ye blest of me and by me - for it is now come when ye shall arise and give unto them that which I shall give unto them thru thee ---

Now I say with authority that I am as one prepared to deliver them from their bondage forever -- Yet I say - they shall do their part - for it is given unto me to see them as ones bowed down with their physical burden - with their puny parts which they have fortuned unto themselves.

I say they shall discipline themself - they shall be as ones on whose shoulders shall rest the responsibility of such parts as the cleaning of the temple and of cleaning of the house - for have I not said that ye shall not have any other work within thy hand? Have I not said that I have prepared thee for this part - why divide thyself?

I say ye have been divided and therein is folly -- When ye took upon thyself thy present physical form - it was for the purpose of doing such as was fortuned unto thee - and ye took such a physical vehicle as was suitable for thy work -- Yet ye waited for a time - wherein ye did many other things in preparation of such work -- Now that ye have been prepared let it pass - for it is not given unto them to be my hand made manifest -- Yet they are servants which I shall reward sufficiently - I say I shall bless them abundantly -- And too I say - there are none great none small within my temple - each unto his own part -- And he shall do his part - and he shall glorify his part by putting of himself into it -- His part shall not be a burden unto him - he shall do it for the joy of serving - and he shall find joy such as he has not known -- So be it he shall be blest by all which come into his presence - for joy shall go out from him ---

Now I say I have spoken on these things for the first time - yet I have said them unto thee before -- Now when it is given unto them in this manner it becomes one of the laws of the temple and none shall say it is not for them -- I say it concerns all which are present and each one which shall come -- So be it each shall do a part and none other shall be responsible for that part - none shall trespass upon the part of the other -- I say - when one comes into this house which I have caused to be set up they shall see order - and peace shall abide therein -- I say all things shall be put into order and nothing which is unclean shall be about it -- Each shall be responsible for his own offal - for his own uncleanliness - and he shall prepare the way for another which is to come -- He shall not break such laws as are set down within this book for I say they have been given unto thee for a purpose which is so vital unto thy own preparation -- I say these laws are thy preparation - and for this have I caused them to be written -- Such is wisdom - blest are they which keep them -- So be it and Selah - I am Sanat Kumara

Sister Thedra of the Emerald Cross

We Have Left Our Home for Their Sake
O - Man - The Shame of Ingratitude to our Benefactors!

Sanat Kumara speaking:

Blest are they which do come into my presence - for I am one sent of God the Father that they may be blest of me and by me - such is my part - and for this have I walked with them -- I have come unto thee that they may receive me - that they may come to know even as I know.

I say - all which do give unto me credit for being that which I am - and unto their preparation due consideration and attention - shall stand within my physical presence -- They shall see me in tangible form - they shall counsel with me - and I shall give unto each his part - which has been prepared for him -- I say he is now preparing himself for yet a greater part -- For this have I given of myself - that they all be freed from their torment and bondage ---

Were it not for thy Benefactors ye should each remain in bondage. Yet we have volunteered to come unto thy rescue - and <u>we have left our homes for thy sake</u> - and as yet ye trouble thyself for such trifles!

I say - ye know not that which ye have forfeited -- I say ye have forfeited a goodly inheritance and I am come that ye may once again claim it -- Such is my will for thee - and I ask of thee: Prepare thyself for such as shall be given unto thee to do ---

So be it that there are days near at hand which shall demand of thee all thy strength - all thy knowing -- all thy wisdom and all thy attention. So be it I shall be by thy side - and I shall sibor thee and I shall sustain thee - yet ye shall be mindful of me - and keep the law which I have given unto thee -- So be it it shall profit thee ---

I am the Grand Worthy Master - Sanat Kumara

Sister Thedra of the Emerald Cross

Trip Not...Many a Slip Twixt the Lip and the Crystal Goblet

Sanat Kumara speaking:-

Beloved of my being: Blest art thou and blest shall ye be - for I am come that ye may be blest -- Was it not said that ye should be unto thyself true -- Have I not said that there would be great trials and temptations - and is it not so -- Have I not said that ye shall not point a finger at another -- Have I not said that there are none so foolish as them which think themself wise -- Have I not given unto thee such laws as shall profit thee -- I say ye shall study them well - and ye shall make them thy own and ye shall do well ---

Be ye as one alert for I say the pitfalls are many -- See that YE trip not - for too I say: There's many a slip twixt the lip and the Crystal Goblet -- I say "There's many a slip twixt the goblet and the lip"---

So be it ye shall make these laws thy own - and forget that the other has tript - should he!

Ye have but the responsibility of thy own preparation - such is thy own responsibility ---

And it is now come when one shall walk among thee as one prepared for that which shall be done within this temple -- I say - one within this temple shall bring forth the new Sibor which shall be as a new born baby fully conscious of his heritage - and fully "---"* cognizant of his being ---

I say - this one which shall bring forth this child shall be as one prepared even as Mary - and which was Mary - and which <u>is</u> Mary - which was the mother of Sananda and which is one and the same -- I say unto thee - ye have given no thought unto these things and ye know not that which is - for ye see the appearance world - ye see not beyond it -- Yet I have said - great things shall be revealed unto thee - I say be ye as ones prepared - for have I not said they shall come to know <u>what is meant by the Virgin</u> - and by the <u>three wise men</u> -- So shall they - and so be it and Selah ---

Now be ye blest of me and by me for I am come that ye may be blest ---

Now I have commanded that the Seal be broken on the word which was brot back from the <u>Temple of the Andes</u> - <u>and when it is brot out ye shall have proof of that which I now say unto thee</u>**-- So be it and Selah ---

I am thy older brother and thy Sibor - Sanat Kumara

Sister Thedra of the Emerald Cross

* Symbol

** Let no man be impatient or hasty to pilfer these Records - Thedra

This is the Testing Ground
When the Sibet is Ready – the Master Will Reveal Himself

Sanat Kumara speaking to thee on certain things which shall profit thee to know - and to put into practice -- I say unto thee that many has been sent into the Earth even as our beloved Brother and Master Sananda - for the purpose of bringing thee out of bondage - and I say unto thee - it is the better part of wisdom to seek them out -- And too I say - as ye prepare thyself to receive them they shall reveal themself unto thee -- I say they reveal themself when ye are prepared for such revelation - such is wisdom ---

Too I say - be ye not deceived by appearances - for appearances are but the veil which stand between thee and reality -- Be ye as ones which can see beyond the veil -- I am one which has been sent of the Father that ye may see -- So be it when ye have sufficiently prepared thyself - I shall personally come unto thee and sibor thee in the way of the wise. So be it for the good of all mankind -- Amen and Selah ---

Now I have given unto thee certain laws or commandments which ye shall follow -- Put them into thy living - make of them thy tools - thy hand maidens - and it shall be unto thee thy key into the place wherein I am - and ye shall be received with great joy and much gladness - I have said this is the testing ground - the proving ground - let it prove thy worth - thy value -- for ones rebellious - full of wonton have no place within this temple -- So be it all thy ways shall be directed in the way ye have set for thyself - be ye not turned aside by appearance or the opinions of others

Bless them which sibor thee - hear that which they have said unto thee -- Be ye prepared for great revelations - for they are being held for the time when ye are prepared to receive them -- I say - we stand with hands tied waiting for thy preparation -- So be it a glad day when we can step forth as we really are and open up the records unto thee ---

Blest shall ye be and glad shall we be - and let it be this day -- Amen and Selah ---

I am thy Brother and thy Sibor - Sanat Kumara

Sister Thedra of the Emerald Cross

For Thy Own Sake - I say
Ye Shall Abide by the Law
Thy Strength Shall be Tested

Sanat Kumara speaking: Blest are they which come unto this altar - and blest shall they be - for I am come that they may be blest -- For have I not set up this altar in the Father's name - and have I not said that I shall be sufficient unto all thy needs -- Have I not commanded of thee great things -- Have I not said unto thee - this is the proving ground -- So it is ---

I am not so foolish as to sibor fools - for I say I am not of a mind to give unto them of myself that they might give unto others that which be unto me my downfall - for I have received my inheritance - and I am not of a mind to forfeit it -- So be it ye shall be wise indeed to <u>be unto thyself true and keep for thyself that which I give unto thee for thy own preparation</u> - for it is for thy own sake that I now speak unto thee thusly. For I say unto thee - there are none so sad as the one which betrays himself or his trust - for I say - they shall begin at the beginning and therein is the pity -- So be as ones which know the law - and for thy own sake I say ye shall abide by it - and let it be forever so ---

Blest are they which come into the place wherein I am and I say unto thee - it is now come when ye shall prove thyself worthy of such for I say - NOT ONE comes into this place unprepared - for there are many keepers of the gates - and they know and know that they know - for they are not deceived by appearance ---

When ye are given such as ye cannot bear - I say unto thee - <u>rejoice within your hearts for the trials which are but thy strength</u> -- I say thy strength shall be tested to the last for this is thy preparation -- I have said this is the proving ground - will it not profit thee to prove thyself sufficient ---

I say ye shall be unto thyself true and ye shall stand as the "Rock" and ye shall not be as the quicksand - and ye shall have within thy hand the Sword of Truth and Justice and ye shall arise to any occasion - and ye shall be as one on whose shoulders rests the responsibility of thy own fortune -- Ye shall not blame another for thy failure nor for thy fortune - for I say ye fortune unto thyself that which ye shall gather unto thyself - Such is the law ---

Be ye as silent as the sphinx and wise as the serpent - for therein is wisdom -- Now too I say unto thee - thou hast not yet begun thy work. This is only thy preparation and it is my part to bring unto thee this part, yet ye shall put into practice that which I have given unto thee in the name of the Father - Son and Holy Ghost - and ye shall be mindful of thy Source of being - and of thy Benefactors - and they shall remember thee in the day of thy trials --

So be it and Selah ---

I am thy Sibor and thy Brother - Sanat Kumara

Sister Thedra of the Emerald Cross

ARISE UNTO THY STATION

Sananda speaking: -

Beloved of my being: I have called thee out of thy bed that this may be written - even thru thy tears -- I say unto thee - it is time that they shall arouse themself from their slumbers - I say they are asleep -- I command of thee greatness in all things - and I say unto thee arise unto thy station and command of them obedience unto the laws which I have caused to be written down -- I give unto thee the authority to say unto them - they shall arise and come forth from their sleep - and they shall be as ones held accountable for thy tears - for I shall hold them accountable for their tears ---

I say they shall arise from their slumbers and they shall put aside their puny ways - their small ego and they shall alert themself and they shall examine themself - and they shall not point a finger at another for they have within their eyes the motes -- Let their vision be clear - for first the mote shall be removed from their own eyes ---

I say they dare not judge one another - for the day of judgement is not theirs and they are not as ones prepared for it -- Too I say - each shall be his own judge and he shall be held accountable unto none other than himself - for there is none other to judge him -- I say - when he has arrived within the Inner Temple he shall be wise - and until then he has not the wisdom to judge - he has not the knowledge which is unto wisdom -- I say he is the foolish one which holds his hand out unto the wind - and says it is but a breeze which bloweth yonder - and he knoweth not whence it cometh ---

Beloved of my soul: Command of them justice - command of them greatness in all their ways -- I say unto thee - be unto them that which I would have thee be -- I say they are worse than asleep - they are dead on their feet -- I say - call them together in my name - give unto them that which I give unto them -- For their sake I have called thee out of thy bed - and I say unto thee I shall make of thee a pillar on which shall stand the Light of the world - I say - upon thy head shall rest a crown such as they have not seen -- So be it and Selah ---

I say ye shall call them together at evening time and at morning time - and they shall be as ones alert - and they shall give of themself and they shall give unto me credit for being that which I am - and I say I am a taskmaster - for I demand obedience and love one for the other.

I say again: None shall point a finger at the other - for he shall go within his own heart and find therein that which he sees within his brothers - and he shall find that which offends him within his own heart and pluck it out - and he shall be unto himself true - and he shall not excuse himself or cast it aside for another day - for he shall this day arise unto the occasion and cleanse his dwelling place - and purify himself - for I say unto thee - it is now come when ye shall stand as a rock - for the time grows short and ye have slept overtime - and ye have given unto thyself credit for being wise when ye have been as the foolish virgins - Ye have had no wisdom - ye have babbled as the foolish - ye have said things which has not been prompted by love - ye have poisoned thy own cup - ye have strewn thy own path with thorns which shall tear thy flesh ---

I say - I am not of a mind to see thee be devoured - and too I say I stand as one with hands tied -- I am now prepared to lay heavy my hand upon thee - and I would that I might spare thee - for ye have not known me nor have ye heard me out - for I am not to be turned out nor am I to be cast aside - for ye have as yet not comprehended that which I am saying unto thee ---

I have caused to be written many things - and I say ye shall study these things which are written - for they have been written for thee - for thy own salvation as part of thy preparation - and I say - when ye are in the temple thy attention shall be given unto the temple work - and if it is given unto thee to be within the world of men - then be unto thy trust true and be unto thy station true - and go out from the temple as one of them and share with them their talents and their darkness -- Yet while ye are given the greater gift and the greater part - why not be mindful of thy blessings - what sayest thou? ---

Be ye as one which has thy eyes folded over with many folds of dark cloth thru which is no light seen -- I say ye are blind as male moles, ye see not that which has been given unto thee -- Ye ask not of the one which I have brot forth for the good of all mankind - that this plan be brot into fruit -- Ye are as ones walking in thy sleep -- We thy Sibors call thee the living dead - we as yet have not reached thee -- I say ye shall arise - ye shall pick thyself up - and ye shall be as ones on whose shoulders rest thy own salvation ---

And ye shall not be unto another a stumbling block - ye shall be unto him a lamp - a living example of an initiate upon the Path -- And I have said - when ye are so prepared I shall send one from out the Inner Temple which shall bring thee in - and I shall be unto myself true - for I shall not fall asleep - as thou hast fallen ---

I say: I am about my Father's business and I am come that ye may awaken - and if I have to put my foot against thy door I shall be sad indeed -- But I have said again and again that none shall enter unprepared - and I shall not deny that which I have said - the law is the law and none are given preference ---

I demand for thee that which I am - and I am one with the Father and I am obedient unto the law - unto every jot and tittle ---

I command of thee - awake and be about the Father's business -- I say it is sad when one faints by the way or turns aside - for these are trying days -- I say ye know not that which I say - for ye are concerned with thy pettiness - thy own self will -- I say ye are as little children playing with toys which ye shall tire of -- Ye shall become weary of the petty things and ye shall call out for relief --

Yet I say ye shall first be obedient unto the laws - for ye shall be as ones which have the will to be brot out of bondage - and therein is thy deliverance - for none come unto thee for the purpose of entertaining thee - it is for thy own sake- and we see thee as ones standing on the brink of destruction and ye know it not -- I too say - the hour swiftly approaches when ye shall be closed out - or ye shall be closed in - in where nothing shall touch thee for is it not written that there is a place prepared for thee wherein nothing shall touch thee in the day of sorrow? I say sorrow there shall be and it is near at hand ---

While we thy Sibors sit at this council table that ye may become aware of that which we say at this table - and of the plan which has been brot forth - ye prattle as the parrots - and ye know not that there are forces building up within the Earth and about the Earth which are accumulating at a great rate each and every moment -- And it is written and wisely so - that the moon shall go out as a wanderling - and the Earth shall flip upon her axis - and I say unto thee - ye sleep on and ye have not stirred in thy sleep -- Pray unto thy God which has given unto thee thy being - for strength and the power that ye shall have need of.

I say all thy petty ways shall be as nothing - ye shall stand face to face with thyself -- Be as one loving and as one lifted up and be unto thyself true - for ye shall not say I have not spoken unto thee with my heart - for I have cried out unto the Father with my being that ye may be brot before that day when the Sun shall be turned into the bowl of blood - and when they shall cry out in agony with the water and fire which shall mingle and which shall be unto them much torment -- I say the fire shall come up out of the oceans and the water shall rain down from the heavens mingled with fire -- I say they - the elements shall be unchained and they shall not obey the command to be still -- I say they shall not obey - for they shall no longer obey a drunken civilization -- They shall no longer be comforted --

I say the Earth shall no longer give footing unto a drunken people. And as for them which has been unto themself true they shall be removed unto a new place of abode - and they shall know no suffering and sorrow - for they shall be the ones chosen - for this shall they prepare themself -- I say they shall now give unto these my words their ear - they shall remember these my words - for they shall be caused to remember them - and they shall do well to read these words until they have come to know that which has been said.

I say unto them: I have called my recorder out of her bed at an hour when they be sleeping - that this paper be prepared for them and I say it shall be sent out unto all which have a mind to follow me -- And too I say - blest are they which do follow me - for I am come that where I go they may go also - so be it the Father's will -- So be it - Amen and Selah ---

I am thy Sibor and thy Brother – Sananda

Sister Thedra of the Emerald Cross

Forewarning Concerning Temple Work

Sanat Kumara speaking:-

I shall add this unto the record which has been read at this altar - and it too shall be added for the benefit of all mankind -- Let it be recorded as I give it - and not one word shall be changed for they shall bear witness of these my words - and they shall see that which I have commanded thee to record ---

I say I am the Grand Worthy Master of this Temple which I have brot forth in the name of the Father - Son and Holy Ghost -- So be it I have come from out the silence that this may be brot forth for the good of all mankind ---

I say ye which are so minded may come unto this altar for the purpose of hearing that which I say unto thee -- Yet I say woe unto anyone which-so-ever casts one stone or which shall point a finger at the one which I have brot forth for the purpose of serving at this altar - I say I am as one accountable for this altar and I shall not allow it to be desecrated - for it is the law that when one sets his hand unto the priest within the temple he sets his hand against the Sword of Justice -- Such is swift and it shall be done in the twinkling of an eye ---

I am mindful of thy weakness and I shall warn thee aforehand - be ye not so foolish as to trespass upon holy ground unprepared -- Be ye as ones prepared and enter therein with joy within thy heart - and be ye mindful of the Source of thy being - and of thy Benefactors which have held thee fast in the hours of thy unknowing ---

Bless them which sibor thee and be ye mindful of the Priestess within the Temple - for I say unto thee - she is my hand made manifest unto thee -- Bless her and give unto her of thy love and of thy strength. Be ye blest for I am come that ye may have Light -- So be it and Selah.

I am thy older Brother - Sanat Kumara

Sister Thedra of the Emerald Cross

As a Man Prepares Himself So He Becomes
Revelation & Preparation

Sananda speaking:-

I say unto thee which is my hand made manifest unto them: Ye shall now say unto them as I would say - that they shall be as ones prepared for that which I have to say unto them - and they shall have upon their own shoulders the responsibility of their preparation -- I say - I can but point the way and they have to walk therein - and too I say that as a man prepares himself so he becomes ---

Now for the first time I say unto thee: I am the Priest within this temple and I have revealed myself for the purpose of giving unto thee Light which shall be sufficient unto the day -- And too I say: Ye shall be as one responsible and as ones grown to maturity -- Ye shall be as ones responsible for all thy own offal - and for thy own reality - and that which is real is not of the dream world - it is neither of the dead or the sleepers realm -- I say I am not among the dead - and I am not asleep - for it is given unto me to see and know that which goes on -- And I am of the Father sent - and I am within the place wherein all things are known and recorded ---

I say unto thee: I have within my hand the power to create like unto the Father - and I say unto thee - I am not a traitor for I know the law - And I say ye which are true unto thyself shall be as ones which shall have great revelation - and ye shall first prove thyself worthy of such revelation - and ye shall be as ones prepared ---

Ye have as yet not comprehended the word revelation - and the word preparation - for ye have not as yet had the proper preparation for such revelation as shall be given unto the just and prudent -- So be it I would give unto thee my inheritance - and I would that I could bring thee in this hour - yet what would that profit thee - ye should be as one kept out for lack of understanding of the law ---

I have given unto the Father my word that I shall bring thee out of bondage - and I am bound until ye have prepared thyself sufficiently that ye may be brot out ---

So be it I ask of thee: prepare thyself for the day is nigh upon thee when ye shall either go out wherein I am and as I go - or ye shall be as one turned back by thy own wonton and by thy own hand -- So be it I shall be sad indeed ---

I am thy older Brother - Sananda

Sister Thedra of the Emerald Cross

Ye Have Not Comprehended the Fullness of Thy Work

Sanat Kumara speaking:-

Beloved of my being: Blest art thou and blest shall ye be - for I am come that ye may be blest ---

Was it not written that ye shall be unto thyself true and give unto the temple work thy undivided attention? - and I say unto thee it is in a deplorable state -- Ye have given of thyself that ye may have the lesser part - yet <u>ye have not comprehended the fullness of thy work</u> - and ye have scattered thy energies - ye have been but like unto children - for ye hear and comprehend not ---

I have said it is my part to give unto thee as ye are prepared to receive - and thy part to walk in the way I point unto thee -- I say ye shall now alert thyself and give unto me credit for knowing that which I say - and knowing that which ye do not ---

I say - we give unto the Father all the credit and the glory -- We are as Sons of God by our own efforts -- For this have we worked - we have willed it so -- So be it and Selah ---

Now ye shall say unto them in my name and as I would say: They shall be as one which has my hand upon them - and they shall be unto themself true - and they shall be as ones blest of me and by me -- So be it and Selah ---

Go from this altar with joy in thy heart - and give unto the Father all the praise and the glory - so be it He shall remember thee -- Amen - so be it ---

I am thy Sibor and thy Brother - Sanat Kumara

Sister Thedra of the Emerald Cross

**When Ye are Properly Prepared
Thy Memory is Sealed Up**

Sanat Kumara speaking:-

Beloved of my being: I am come that ye may receive of the Father as I have received - and for this shall ye be prepared - I say as ye prepare thyself so shall ye receive ---

Too it is written and wisely so - that none come into the place wherein I am unprepared -- I say I AM - and I am within a place -- I am not an imaginary figure - I AM - and because the Father IS - I AM and He has given unto me my inheritance in full - and I am glad - I know such joy as ye know not of -- I say for this is the way the Father has willed unto me - that I might come unto thee that ye might be brot out of thy bondage - in love - mercy and in wisdom ---

I say it is the better part of wisdom to receive us - in love and with an open heart - than the wandering which ye have chosen

I say of thy own free will have ye gone into darkness - and of my own free will have I given of myself that ye may be brot out

Now I would give unto thee this day this word: When ye are properly prepared - I shall step forth and as one in flesh and bone and I shall touch thee with my hand - which ye shall be able to feel and touch as even ye can touch any other -- And I shall call forth the elements and I shall command of them to obey thee - and this shall be done in the presence of one which is known unto us as Sananda ---

I say unto thee: These laws are not revealed unto the unjust or to the IMPRUDENT - for we are not so foolish as to betray ourself - for we have been diligent in our part -- And I say - I have spoken unto thee in wisdom and with love -- I am a merciful man - I am of the Father sent that ye may receive thy freedom from all bondage ---

Be ye as one which has the mind to comprehend that which I say and it shall profit thee -- I ask of thee: Pray for thy memory - wherein is stored all knowledge - for therein is wisdom ---

I say thy memory is sealed up - and too I say it shall be broken and I am glad -- I say ye shall pray for thy memory - and ye shall receive - And have I not said: "I shall stand before the Great White Altar within this mountain and declare for thee thy freedom?" So be it and Selah.

I am thy Sibor and thy Brother - Sanat Kumara

Sister Thedra of the Emerald Cross

Crown of The Sun
Seal of Solomon

Sananda speaking: -

Beloved of my being: Blest are they which come unto this altar which the Father has set up -- I say unto thee - blest are they which come unto the Source of all knowledge - and ask of God the Father that they may be learned of Him -- And as they ask of Him - He sends one of His own out that they may receive that which He has willed unto them -- Now will it so that ye shall be brot into the place wherein I am and I say unto thee great shall be thy revelation and ye shall be glad for thy preparation

Now let it be said that one shall come unto thee in the name of the Father - Son and Holy Ghost - and he shall lead thee into the place wherein stands the great White Altar of Alabaster - and ye shall stand before it and I shall declare for thee thy freedom - and ye shall be glad for thy preparation -- Now be ye as one foretold - for ye shall know the one which shall come unto thee - for it is written and wisely so - that his countenance shall be so bright ye cannot look upon it -- So be it and Selah ---

Now was it not said that one should come unto thee - and have I not said that he shall come in the name of the Father - Son and Holy Ghost? I declare unto thee - one shall come unto thee from out the Inner Temple and he shall be as none other - for he shall have upon his head the Crown of the Sun - and upon his forehead the Seal of Solomon - and ye shall know him for he shall be as none other - and I say ye shall be blest by him and of him ---

Now be ye as ones prepared to receive him in the name of the Father, Son and Holy Ghost - so shall there be much gladness and great joy -- Blest are they which receive him -- So be it and Selah ---

Now let it be recorded that they which do go unto the White Mountain on the day ahead - shall be as ones blest - for they shall be as ones which have my hand upon them - and they shall prepare themself for that which shall be given unto them -- I say ye shall go as one prepared to record that which I shall say unto them - for I shall speak unto them and they shall heed that which I say - so be it it shall profit them -- I am with thee and I shall remember thee -- So be it and Selah.

Blest art thou and blest shall they be which hear that which I say.

I am thy Brother and thy Sibor - Sananda

Sister Thedra of the Emerald Cross

Sibors of The Royal Assembly

Sanat Kumara speaking:-

Blest are they which come to this altar and blest shall they be -- And I say unto thee - ye shall be as ones which have my hand upon thee - for great is the need for them which have the will to serve within the plan which has been brot forth for this new day - and for this new dispensation -- Yet I say unto thee: Ye have dragged thy legirons with thee from past ages - and they have been unto thee great weight and have held thee within thy tracks bound -- I say ye have not been freed as yet from thy bondage -- Yet let it be said again - that we thy Sibors of the Royal Assembly have come that ye may be freed -- I say AGAIN and AGAIN - YE HAVE NOT KNOWN THE MEANING OF FREEDOM -- I say ye are in bondage - ye are bound by such laws as ye have fortuned unto thyself - and ye have been in darkness for lo many eons - ye have not remembered thy inheritance willed unto thee of the Father ---

Now I say - it is come when ye which have the will to remember shall be quickened - and ye shall give unto me credit for knowing that which I say -- Ye shall be quickened and ye shall remember all things. Ye shall know even as we know for it is the Father's will -- I say He is a generous Father - He is merciful - and He has willed unto thee His vast Estate -- He has willed unto us - <u>You</u> and <u>Me</u> - all that He has - all that He is - and be ye as one prepared to receive it ---

Now I say ye shall prepare thyself for such as He has willed unto thee -- And He has gone the long way with thee - for He has waited long for thy return -- I say ye have gone out from Him - and to Him shall ye return ---

Blest are they which do return - for they shall go into darkness no more -- And I say they shall know no sorrow - I say they shall receive their own Godhood ---

Blest am I for I have received my inheritance in full - and I come unto thee that ye may receive of the Father as I have received - so be it every man's inheritance ---

I am now prepared to come unto thee and to give unto thee as I have received of them which have gone before me -- And when ye are so prepared I shall come unto thee as one in tangible form - and I shall give unto thee a part which is strange and new unto thee - and I say I shall reveal many things unto thee -- So be it that ye shall be glad for thy preparation -- Be ye blest even as I am blest ---

I am thy Sibor and thy Elder Brother - Sanat Kumara

Sister Thedra of the Emerald Cross

In Unity There is Strength

Be ye as one blest of me - for I have seen thee within the place wherein ye are as one which has a mind to learn -- And now I say unto thee: Ye shall be as one which has my hand upon thee - and ye shall say unto them in my name - that they shall be as one man - for they shall have need of their strength - and they shall be as ones which have the responsibility of their own preparation -- And I say that they shall be as "ONE" for in unity there is strength -- And I say ye shall stand as one man - for therein is wisdom ---

And it is now come when there shall be one among thee which shall be as <u>one sent out from the den of the dragon</u> -- And that one shall deny me - for that one shall be as none other - for it is given unto that one to serve the forces of darkness - and to serve the fallen one -- When ye have joined thyself together as one man under the banner of Truth and Justice - not one shall prevail against thee - for I say: In unity is strength.

Now - were it not so dark within the Earth - we thy Sibors and Benefactors should wait for yet another day - when the efforts of the illumined ones would be of less strain - I say it would be the easier part. <u>Yet there is a great necessity to bring forth the martyred saints -</u> and the illumined ones from other realms - that there might be enough light within the Earth - that sufficient balance may be brot about to keep the Earth on her course - and for this do we work at this time -- I say we have worked diligently that the Earth and the children thereof may be delivered out of darkness - out of bondage -- I say unto thee: Love ye one another and ye shall be blest of me and by me -- And let it suffice that I am thy older Brother - and call me The Nameless One -- So let it be ---

I am One Sent of God the Father -- I come from out the Silence -- so shall I speak again and again -- So be it and Selah -- Blessings forevermore ---

Sister Thedra of the Emerald Cross

One of Sananda's best maxims:

"It has been said: The tongue is the devil's best weapon - Why not disarm him?"

Obedience Necessary

Sanat Kumara speaking: -

Blest art thou and blest shall ye be -- Ye shall this day go into solitude with thy "---" and ye shall be given a part which has been prepared for thee - and ye shall wait for a time wherein ye shall be blest of Me and ye shall be as one - for I say ye shall go into solitude within the place wherein the last part was given - for another part shall be given as that one - When it is done the one which has given the place shall be called - and likewise the one which is now absent -- I say the one which is now absent shall sit with thee in the place of seclusion - and too I say: While ye are gone from this temple wherein ye are - it shall be prepared for thy return - and that which ye have received shall be given unto them -- So be it it shall profit them ---

Now I say - ye shall go straitway within the hour - and ye shall be as one obedient to the command - and ye shall wait for a time for thy blessing ---

I say - go straitway within the hour and ye shall go from this altar in silence into that place and with thee shall go the one on thy right side. He too shall go in silence ---

I am with thee and I shall be with thee to the end ---

Blest art thou and blest are they which gather about this altar which has been brot forth thru the Great White Star -- Allejua - Allejua --

Preparation for the Great White Altar - Holy Mt.

Sananda speaking:-

Be ye at peace and blest shall ye be -- And seek ye the Light of the Christ for ye shall be as one on whose shoulders rests great responsibility ---

And it is now come when one among thee shall be given a part which shall be new and which shall be unto him a great responsibility for in the time which is near - he shall be brot before the Great White Altar for the purpose of gaining wisdom - and there shall be a place for him in which he shall serve as one which has been prepared ---

And now - when ye have called them together ye shall read this my testimony unto them - and they shall remember these my words - and they shall be as ones which have the will to hear that which I say unto them -- So be it it shall profit them ---

For the first time I say unto thee - one shall go out from among thee as one prepared for a new part - and that one shall stand before the Great White Altar within the Holy Mountain wherein ye are and he shall be as one prepared for the greater part -- So be it and Selah ---

I am now come that he shall be alerted and prepared -- So be it and Selah ---

With my own hand I shall bless him ---

I am thy older Brother - Sananda

Sister Thedra of the Emerald Cross

The Prodigal
(Ye have had thy Memory Blanked from Thee)

Sanat Kumara speaking: -

Beloved which has come unto the altar of Gods which have within them the fortune willed unto them of our Father - which is every man's inheritance -- I say it is every man's inheritance to be a Son of God - a God within his own divinity - and so let it by the Grace and Love of the Father which has given unto us being -- So be it - Amen and Selah ---

I say unto thee: ye have gone out from the Father as one perfect - and unto Him shall ye return perfect even as ye went out -- Yet ye shall be as one which have prepared thyself for thy return ---

I say unto thee: Ye have had thy memory blanked from thee - and it is now come when ye shall will that it be restored unto thee -- And if and when ye ask of the Father that it be restored - one shall be sent unto thee for the purpose of being unto thee His hand made manifest - and ye shall be glad to receive Him and to receive of Him - for He shall declare for thee thy freedom ---

So be it it shall profit thee to ask of the Father thy freedom - and again I say - He shall hear thee - and ye shall not be turned away -- And He shall receive thee unto Himself with much gladness and great joy such as ye have not known ---

Blest are they which do return unto the Father - for they shall receive of Him their Godhood -- Such is thy inheritance - such is the Father's Love and Mercy - and ye shall profit by thy preparation -- I say ye shall be blest for I am come that ye may be blest ---

Now I say unto thee at this altar - that one shall come unto thee and he shall direct thee - and ye shall be as one prepared to receive him -- Now let it be recorded thusly: Ye shall receive one at this altar which shall be sent from out the Great White Mountain wherein stands the Altar of White Alabaster - and he shall be unto thee much Light and give unto thee great revelation - for I say ye shall be unto thyself true - and ye shall be prepared to receive Him and He shall know thee as ye are --

He will not be deceived for He has been well trained for this part- Now be ye as ones which have my hand upon thee and I shall bless thee and I shall follow after the first one -- Such is my preparation - for I have become that for which I have prepared myself - and I have received my inheritance in full -- So be it and Selah ---

I Am thy older Brother and thy Sibor - Sanat Kumaran

Sister Thedra of the Emerald Cross

When Shall the Lord Reveal Himself?

Father-Mother God - Benefactors: I - Thedra come to this altar which You have set up - for the good of all mankind -- Let it be known unto me this day how I can better serve Thee and the Plan You have brot forth -- I bring myself as a living sacrifice -- Use me as You will -- Glorify Thyself in me - and thru me - and cause me to walk in the Light of the Christ forever and forever -- So be it as Thou hast willed it ---

Sananda speaking: -

Beloved of my being: I say unto thee this morning: As I have given unto thee so shall ye give unto them -- I say ye shall give unto them which are of a mind to receive that which I have given unto thee for them - that they may have Light ---

And is it not written and wisely so - that I am now in the Earth prepared to reveal myself unto them which are prepared to receive me and of me - I say - they which do give unto me credit for being that which I am - and for being the Son of God - Sent as such and fortuned to be the One which comes in His name for the purpose of bringing unto the Earth Light - which is thy deliverance from all bondage - then and only then shall I reveal myself unto them ---

I speak unto them which sit within the places of darkness wherein they are bound - wherein they serve the forces of darkness -- I say they which labor for bread shall see that which binds them - and that which has been unto them the millstone about their neck -- I say they shall see that which has been unto them their legirons - and they shall be as ones which have a mind to turn from it and to seek the light ---

They shall flee from that which has bound them and they shall call for the light - for knowledge of their being -- They shall seek the Light which is eternal and wherein all things are known - wherein is no mystery -- I say that which has mystified thee shall no longer be a mystery - for all things shall be revealed unto them which purifies themself and are found to be worthy and prudent ---

I say - We thy Sibors are not so foolish as to sibor traitors and fools for therein would we be betraying our trust and ourself ---

Blest are they which are found worthy ---

I am come that ye may have Light - yet I say ye shall prepare thyself for such revelation as shall profit thee -- So be it and Selah ---

I am One Sent of God the Father - and He which was once called Jesus of Nazareth - now known in the Temple of Light as Sananda --

Sister Thedra of the Emerald Cross

Who Shall See God Face to Face?

Sanat Kumara speaking:-

Blest are they which come unto this altar in the name of The Most High Living God -- I say they shall be blest of Him and by Him ---

Blest are they which have received my words and which abide by that which has been given unto them - as the part which shall be unto them their preparation -- I say - blest are they which prepare themself for the greater part - I say they shall walk and talk with me - and they which walk with me shall see God face to face -- So be it and Selah ---

I say this is the greater part - and for this has He - The Father sent me unto thee that I may bring thee out of darkness - such is my part - and it is thy part to prepare thyself for the greater part ---

Now I ask for thy freedom - I declare for thee thy freedom--

Now have ye been as diligent - have ye willed it so?

Have ye watched thy tongue - thy every thot?

Have ye been in the place of the publicans?

Have ye floundered in shallow waters?

Have ye slept on thy feet?

Have ye remembered what has been said in this house of

God - at this Altar?

Have ye given unto my hand made manifest the credit due?

Have ye waited by the wayside for the thief which would pick thy pocket and slap thy face?

Have ye been watchful of thy own way - how can ye sleep upon thy feet?

I say ye as yet have not applied the laws which have been given unto thee -- And too I say - be ye not dismayed - for the sincerity of purpose is a great treasure to be held within thy heart - and none shall take that from thee -- And too have I not said - I see thee as ye are and not as ye appear to be --

I say there is a law which I am one with - that shall be revealed in this age - and for this do I claim for thee thy freedom -- And while it is yet time I ask of thee: Let no words pass from thy lips which would bind thee - for each word is that which would free thee - or bind thee. I say ye know not the power of the spoken word - be as a guardian of them - for as the fowls of the air they return unto their resting places - and great shall be the joy thereof - or the stench -- Be ye not so foolish as to dung thy place of abode -- I have said: "Unto the waters I dung - I purify"---

Blest are they which have ears to hear - let him hear - and let him be the one to cleanse himself and receive of the Water of Life - so be it he shall go into darkness no more -- Amen and Selah -- Sanat Kumara

Sister Thedra of the Emerald Cross

Such Knowledge is not Available to the Unjust

Sanat Kumara speaking:-

Beloved of my being: Blest art thou for I have lifted thee up - I have brot thee into the place wherein I am -- And I have given unto thee a portion which ye have sealed up - and which shall be opened for all to see and know at a later time -- When they have been prepared for such a portion - I say it shall be revealed unto them -- And too I say: No man <u>can</u> pilfer such knowledge - it has been written and recorded for thee - that they shall not eat of this Tree of Knowledge --

I say ye get not such knowledge by the food of thy mouth - ye get not such knowledge by the reading of such books as ye have acquired, ye have not such knowledge available unto the unjust and the imprudent -- I say - ye do not acquire such knowledge as is revealed thru the Source of thy being --

And it is the law - when ye acquire such knowledge it is by and thru revelation -- I say - revelation is a gift of God The Father - willed unto thee as part of thy inheritance -- And ye shall now give unto the Father credit for thy being - and unto thy Benefactors credit for that which they are - and unto them credit for thy well-being - and unto thyself credit for being a Son of God ---

And love thyself and ye shall be as one blest of the Father - Son and Holy Ghost -- Amen -- So be it and Selah ---

Go thy way this day rejoicing that it is now come that ye shall have within thy hand the POWER to receive that which has been willed unto thee - and I say that power shall be revealed unto thee in the name of the Father - Son and Holy Ghost --

It has been written and wisely so - that no man climbeth up any other way - and so it is -- And so be it that any man which pilfers such knowledge is a thief and shall not enter into the kingdom of God -- So be it that ye shall come by the way set before thee -- I am come that ye may be brot in - in love - harmony and in dignity -- I say ye shall return unto the place of thy going out in dignity.

So be it and Selah ---

I am thy Elder Brother - Sanat Kumara

Sister Thedra of the Emerald Cross

Excerpts:

"Love thy life which is endowed unto thee of the Father - and thy freedom is assured thee"--

From the Sibors Teachings Thru Sister Thedra

Ye Shall Not be Bound Against Thy Will

Sananda speaking:-

Be ye blest of my presence and of my being: I say unto thee I am with thee - and I say I AM - for the Father has sent me unto thee that ye may have thy inheritance which He has willed unto thee ---

Now my children I say unto thee as He the Father would say: There are none so sad as he which would betray himself - and too I say: There are none to bind thee against thy will -- I say ye shall not be bound against thy will -- And too I say: Ye have willed all thy woe - and sorrow - and it is now come when ye shall will for thyself the greater things -- I say ye shall be as ones which have reached the age of maturity - and ye shall walk as men and ye shall not be afraid - for I say no man shall decree for thee thy bondage - for I have come that ye be brot out of bondage -- And I say unto thee - I am not of a mind to come into the places wherein the porcupines dwell - I say I am not so foolish for I go not into the den of the porcupines - for they are not prepared to receive me ---

Now I say unto thee: Ye shall rest at peace and be ye at poise - for I am saying unto thee that they know not when they say ye are surrounded by the porcupines -- Be ye not deceived - nor be ye afraid - have I not given thee my word - I should go before thee that nothing evil or of darkness should overtake thee -- I am not asleep nor am I in lethargy -- So be it my patience is strained -- So be it my love exceeds my patience -- So be it ye shall try my patience again and again - yet I shall bear with thee a while longer - yet ye shall not mock me ---

I am thy Sibor and thy Brother - Sananda

Sister Thedra of the Emerald Cross

Excerpts:

"Give unto me credit for being that which I am - and give unto Me credit for knowing that which I say unto thee - and I shall give unto thee the part which I have kept for thee"--

-Sananda

Ye Shall be prepared Aforehand

Sanat Kumara speaking:-

Be ye blest of my presence - and I say unto thee ye shall be as ones which have my hand upon thee - and ye shall walk upon thy feet as man for it is now come when ye shall be brot out of darkness and ye shall will it so - so shall it be -- I say ye shall will it so - and so be it ---

Now let this be recorded this day - that I shall take from this place one which I have brot in - and too I say - ye shall be as ones which have gone the long way that this may be accomplished -- Ye shall wonder at these my words - yet ye shall have them at thy finger tips - for ye shall be caused to remember them ---

Now ye shall refer to thy Bible for the purpose of reminding thyself that there are times when things are given unto thee aforehand which ye do not comprehend at the time -- I say ye are prepared aforehand - so be it the better part of wisdom ---

I am now prepared to give unto thee the greater part -- Ye shall prepare thyself to receive it ---

I am thy Sibor and thy older Brother - Sanat Kumara

Sister Thedra of the Emerald Cross

Great Responsibility Goes with Ordination

Sanat Kumara speaking: -

Blest art thou and blest are they -- I say ye shall be blest of me and by me - for I come that ye may be blest -- So be it and Selah ---

Now for the first time I say unto thee: Ye shall have none of the misery which is fortuned unto them - for I shall be unto thee a Shield and a Buckler ---

Be ye as one prepared for that which I shall give unto thee to do - for in the time which is near I shall call upon thee for a part which is new and strange unto thee and ye shall respond in haste - such is obedience and such is wisdom ---

Now let it be said that ye have been obedient in all things and ye have answered every call - and with my own hand have I directed thee. Now I shall give unto thee a part which shall prepare thee that ye may lead them even as I have led thee -- And it has now come when they too shall step forth and take up the yoke - and be as ones which can assume such responsibilities as goes with such an ordination - for it is the times which has been prophesied when every man shall stand - and as one - fight shoulder to shoulder or he shall perish as with a great blast from out the north - I say as with a great blast from out the north.

Ye have as yet no concept of my words and their meaning - yet I say - as one shall ye stand or perish - for within the world of man are many which have the will to overcome all thy good works and all thy knowing -- I say they are the agents of the fallen one - and they shall be put down -- And too I say - ye are as the emissaries of Light - and it is required of thee this day to hold the Light of the Christ in balance - that even the Elements shall obey thy loving command -- And I say unto thee: Watch every word which procedes from thy mouth - and ye have gone a long way when ye have mastered thy tongue -- So be it a battle won ---

I am now with thee for the purpose of giving unto thee that which shall profit thee - and ye shall either accept it or reject it -- And blest are they which shall use it for their own sake ---

I am thy older Brother and thy Sibor - Sanat Kumara

Sister Thedra of the Emerald Cross

He Shall Carry Within His Hand - A Goblet

Sanat Kumara speaking: -

Beloved of my being: Blest art thou - and blest are they which come unto this altar which the Father has set up -- So be it in His name - Amen and Selah -- Now it is come when ye have gone out - and to Him the Father shall ye return -- I say - ye shall return unto Him even as ye went out - perfect as in the beginning ---

For the first time I say unto thee: Ye have this day earned the right to call thyself a Son of God the Father - for ye have been given thy inheritance in full -- Ye have not accepted it and for this shall ye prepare thyself - for it is now come when many shall come unto thee for the purpose of gaining wisdom -- And I say ye shall be as one prepared for thy new part which has been prepared for thee -- And I say unto thee: As ye prepare thyself so shall ye receive - and this is the law: As a man prepares himself so shall he become ---

Now it is given unto me to see them running to and fro - looking about them for the solution of all their woes - yet they find no solution for they look in the places of darkness - and therein is no wisdom -- I say - they have not sought the Source of their being - nor have they asked of the Source -- I say they go about within the world of men as ones lost - they know not whither they goest - neither do they remember their Source of being - and therein is the pity -- Blest are they which seek their Source - and blest shall they be ---

I am come that ye may have thy inheritance given unto thee in full. I say ye shall accept it in the name of the Father - Son and Holy Ghost. Amen and Selah ---

For the first time I say: One shall come unto thee with his credentials within his hand - for he shall carry within his hand a Goblet a Crystal Goblet of which I have spoken many times -- And I say - when ye see that Goblet within his hand - ye shall ask that ye may drink and I say - when ye do drink of the water from the Crystal Goblet - ye shall step forth from the dense form of physical substance - into the body of light substance which shall be thy <u>whole</u> body - thy Holy Body, the Christ Body - which shall not bind thee -- And ye shall be free from the gravitation of the Earth and free from the attraction of the moon -- Such is thy inheritance and even more - I say ye shall return unto them as one prepared to lift the dead - heal the sick and to cast out daemons Such shall be part of thy part - such is he which has received the greater part -- Blest is he which has the greater part for he shall have within his hand all power - and he shall be one with it -- He shall be trustworthy in all things -- He shall have the power to create like unto the Father - and he shall have the wisdom which is given of the Father -- Such is the Father's Will -- So be it and Selah ---

I am thy older Brother and thy Sibor - Sanat Kumara

Sister Thedra of the Emerald Cross

Preparation for Ascension
Before the White Altar

Sanat Kumara speaking: -

Beloved of my being: Be ye blest of my presence and of my being for I am come that ye may be blest -- So be it in the name of the Most High Living God -- Amen -- So be it I am in the place wherein I shall declare for thee thy freedom - and I say unto thee - there are none within this place which are not prepared for the part which they have -- And too I say - that there are fourteen within this place wherein stands the great White Altar of Alabaster - and wherein stands the Priest which is our beloved Brother Sananda -- I say we have gathered ourself within this I place for the purpose of giving unto certain ones a part for which they have waited -- I say that there are three within this place this day which are now being prepared for their ascension-- I say that we have been brot into this place for the purpose of giving assistance unto these brothers ---

And too I say - it is not new unto us for we are about the Father's business -- And we are not unaware of our part and of the inheritance willed unto us of the Father -- So be it that I am now prepared to bring thee in and to give unto thee as we have received -- So be it and Selah.

I say - ye shall now give unto them this part - and they shall hear from my own lips that which I say - and as it is plainly written and well recorded that they may have knowledge of such as they have not known. I say they shall come to know such - that which goes on within the realm of Light ---

Now I say unto thee: Some shall be filled with opinions - some shall say Nay! Nay! And so shall it be - as they are prepared - for I say unto thee - there are none so foolish as the one which thinks himself wise - and none so sad as he which betrays himself -- So be ye as wise as the serpent and silent as the sphinx - I say boast not of thy knowledge - for ye have not as yet heard or seen that which ye shall see or hear -- I say ye shall come to know that which has been hidden from thee -- So be it and Selah ---

I am with thee and I shall be with thee unto the end -- So be it and Selah ---

I am thy Sibor and thy Brother - Sanat Kumara

Sister Thedra of the Emerald Cross

I am Not so Foolish as to Sibor Fools & Traitors

Sanat Kumara speaking: Blest are they which come to this altar and blest shall they be -- Now let it be recorded that as a man prepareth himself so shall be become -- I say he becomes that for which he prepares himself -- No man cometh into the place wherein I am unprepared -- So be it and Selah ---

Be ye as one which has my hand upon thee and I shall lead them into the place wherein I am - and I shall bless thee as I have been blest. So be it ye shall receive even as I have received of God the Father -- So be it -- Amen and Selah ---

Blest are they which do receive as I have received - and blest shall they be -- And it is my part to prepare thee to receive as I have received yet ye shall do thy part - and ye shall walk in the way set before thee - Such is thy preparation - and when ye are so prepared I shall come unto thee and counsel thee even as I am -- And have I not said that I shall come into the world of flesh even as ye are -- Of flesh and bone shall I come - and I shall sup with thee and I shall speak unto thee in words which ye can hear and comprehend - and ye shall know as I know - for I shall cause thee to comprehend ---

I am prepared for such an occasion - and I am not so foolish as to sibor fools and traitors -- I say I do not sibor the foolish for I am not of them and they are not of Me - for they have not prepared themself to receive Me -- So be it I shall keep my word and I have said it -- So be it -- Amen and Selah ---

I am thy Sibor and thy older Brother - Sanat Kumara

Ye Shall Present Thyself in a Befitting Manner

Sananda speaking: Blest are they which come unto this altar which the Father has set up -- And I say unto thee He has willed for thee a place wherein ye shall be brot in the time which is near -- And I say ye have as yet not begun thy work - for as yet ye have not prepared thyself for the greater part - yet it is time that ye be prepared ---

And I say that one shall present himself unto thee when ye are prepared to receive Him -- And too I say ye shall present thyself at this altar in a befitting manner - and ye shall give unto Me thy undivided attention - and ye shall be reminded of thy shortcomings - for they are many - and I shall remind thee again and again -- I say ye shall come unto this altar in a befitting manner and ye shall prepare thyself aforehand and come as ye would - should ye enter into the Citadels of the world ---

I say ye have been as ones which have not the mind of the elite and ye have been lax in thy ways -- Ye have been thotless of Me and My presence -- Be ye as ones respectful of thy Benefactors and of thy own self - for I am with thee and I demand respect in all things - so be ye as ones reminded -- So be it I shall speak unto thee again on this subject.

I am thy older Brother and thy Sibor - Sananda

Sister Thedra of the Emerald Cross

New Dispensation

Sanat Kumara speaking:-

Blest art thou and blest are they which come unto this altar which has come into manifestation in the name of the Father - Son and Holy Ghost -- So be it that all which do come shall be blest -- Amen and Selah ---

I am now prepared to bring thee into the place wherein I am and to give unto thee as I have received -- So be it that I have received my inheritance in full -- Amen and Selah ---

Be ye as one which can comprehend the laws which have been set before thee and abide by them - and ye have but to walk in the way set before thee ---

I say - wall ye in the way set before thee and ye shall profit thereby. Blest are they which abide by laws given unto them -- And too I say - ye have been given a new dispensation and a new law - for ye are now privileged to come the easy and safer way - for many have come into the Earth that ye may have help - that ye may be brot out in this day -- And too I say - ye are no longer of the old order - ye are under a new law - and a new dispensation has been given unto thee - and ye have as yet not comprehended that which is being done that ye may have thy freedom while it is yet time --

For the great day draweth near when there shall be great torment and great sorrow - for within the Earth and about the Earth is great source of darkness which shall come forth into manifestation -- And I say that it is NECESSARY that ye get into the proper place wherein ye are to work within the plan - and then when ye have been assigned thy place - ye shall give unto it thy whole time without exception and with joy and with dignity --

And I say it shall be an example to all people - for within these places - I say within these temples which shall be set up - we do give explicit instructions which are for thy own good and for the good of all mankind -- I say we are not so foolish as to betray ourself or our trust. And I say - if the sibet should turn aside - that another shall be brot out to fill his place - yet pity shall he be which does turn aside ---

I am now come that this plan shall be fulfilled -- So shall it be - Amen and Selah ---

My Father has entrusted unto me this part and I have come voluntarily - and I shall see it thru unto the end - such is my word unto thee -- I am of the Order of Melchizedek - which I have spoken of - and I say unto thee ye are of the Order of Melchizedek and of the Order of Sarah - and there are certain Brothers which shall guard and be unto thee shields from the world - and I say they shall be called the "Sons of Sarah"- for they have been given the Seal of Sarah and they shall carry with them a seal which shall be given unto them - and they shall be aware at all times of their sacred responsibility --

And too I say - it is a <u>most</u> <u>sacred</u> responsibility - and it is given unto me to know -- And woe unto any man which defiles his <u>sister</u> - for he has upon his heart a seal and that seal shall be broken and he shall see himself as he is -- And he shall know that which is - which was - and which shall be -- I say he shall be as one come alive - and he shall know that all things are his - and he shall not transgress one law without paying dearly -- Poor in spirit is he which transgresses a law knowingly, and pity is he which knows not - for he is in darkness ---

Blest is he which is brot out of darkness - and his reward shall be great indeed -- Blest am I to be privileged to come unto thee -- So be it I am glad ---

I am thy older Brother and thy Sibor - Sanat Kumara

Sister Thedra of the Emerald Cross

The Great White Mountain
The White Alabaster Altar

Sananda speaking unto thee at this hour: - There are ones from the realms of Light gathered together at the altar within the heart of the Great White Mountain wherein stands the White Altar of Alabaster - which do come together for the good of all mankind - and so be it -- It is in the name of the Most High Living God ---

Now I have said unto thee that one shall stand before this altar and declare for thee thy freedom -- I say that one now stands within this place wherein there are ones from three temples which have come from out the realms of Light -- They come that the law might be filled - that the Earth may give up her secrets -that the ones so prepared may be brot in and given the part which has been kept for them ---

Now I say that there are many from the world of men which shall be found and brot out from them - which shall be brot in and given a new part - and which shall go out again as ones prepared for a new part. And I say ye shall be given as ye are prepared to receive ---

Now let it be said ye have come into this place - even within this building wherein ye are - for the purpose of serving within this plan which is now unfolding before thee -- And I say ye have not yet begun thy great work which is yet to be revealed unto thee -- I say as yet the greater part has not been revealed unto thee ---

I too say that when ye are prepared ye shall receive even as I have received and ye shall be glad for thy preparation ---

I have said: This is the path of initiation - so it is and so be it in the name of the Father - Son and Holy Ghost -- Amen and Salah ---

I am within this place prepared to bring thee in and to give unto thee a part which is yet to be revealed unto thee - and I say there are none so foolish as he which thinks himself wise - and none so sad as he which betrays himself or his trust ---

Be ye as ones true unto thyself and I shall bring thee into the place wherein we now sit in council for thy own benefit -- I say we have received our inheritance in full - yet ye have forfeited thy own -- So shall ye have it returned unto thee as ye are prepared ---

Now for the first time I say unto thee that one in this place has come from a far and distant galaxy wherein is no darkness -- And for this Holy event and on this occasion which is new unto thee - have they been sent of the Father that there may be a close tie or bond between that planet or galaxy and that of thy own - I say that this is the occasion for great joy and much rejoicing ---

Too I say ye have not as yet learned the secrets of the initiate which ye shall come to know - and for this do ye prepare thyself ---

Too it is said and wisely so that none find their way into this place with measuring rod and tape - and neither do they come unprepared - for they have to have the proper credentials -- And I say we are not fools or traitors - for we know thee even as ye are - and I say ye shall come clean of hands and of heart - for ye have but to cleanse thyself of all thy lusts - all thy rebelliousness (wonton) - and of all thy hatreds - all thy jealousy - all thy pettiness - and forever free thyself of thy own legirons which ye drag after thee -- And I say from this day forward shall we watch thee as one which has presented thyself for admittance within this temple ---

And as I have said unto thee many times: "Unto the waters I dung I purify"- so be it the better part of wisdom ---

I am thy older Brother and thy Sibor - Sananda

Initiation

Sananda speaking unto thee:-

Be ye blest of me and by me - and be ye as one upon which I lay my hand and I shall lift thee up and I shall bless thee - and I come unto that ye may be blest -- For it is now come when ye shall go out into all the lands of the Earth - and ye shall touch them and ye shall heal them of all manner of infirmities - and for this are ye being prepared -- So be it I am with thee and I shall not forsake thee - for I forsake not my own.

I am within the place wherein I am prepared to come unto thee and to give unto thee a part which is new unto thee and ye shall be as one prepared to receive it -- So be it and Selah---

I say unto thee: They shall be blest of Me and by Me - such is my word unto thee -- Amen - So be it and so shall it be - Let it be ---

I have spoken and my word shall not return unto Me void -

I am Sananda

Sister Thedra of the Emerald Cross

When Thy Memory is Restored

Sanat Kumara speaking: -

Blest art thou and blest are they which come unto this altar which the Father has set up - for they shall be blest of Him - for it is now come when they shall be brot out from among them - and they shall find within themself that for which they have sought ---

I say they have run hither and yon looking for that which they know not - and they have found no peace -- Now it is come when peace shall be established within them - for I say we - thy Sibors have come that there might be peace -- I say we bring not peace - yet we make way for peace -- Blest are they which do find it ---

Now when ye are so prepared - one shall come unto thee and he shall touch thee and ye shall know the Peace which is His - and ye shall be blest of Him - and by Him -- Such is his part to come unto thee and open up thy memory - and ye shall know as he knows -- Ye shall remember thy being - and thy time <u>before ye went into darkness</u> -- <u>Ye shall remember thy being which was before thy going out from the Father - thy day before going into bondage</u> -- <u>Ye shall know that which is meant by freedom and love</u>-- <u>Ye shall know the law governing all things - and ye shall be free forevermore - and ye shall go into bondage no more</u> -- Such is his part - and it is thy part to prepare thyself to receive him -- And I say unto thee he is not a fool - for he has the fortune to know thee as ye are - and he goes not out on a fool's mission nor does he be deceived by appearances ---

I am now prepared to receive them into the place wherein I am when they are prepared to come -- Wherein I am are fourteen - and when they are prepared for to be brot in - this place shall be ablaze with the lights which shall come in -- For it is the plan that when the next one is brot in - that a sign shall appear within the sky and they shall see it from afar -- And I say unto thee - ye shall prepare thyself for ye may be given a sign which ye have not seen and which ye know not -- Yet ye shall remember these my words and ye shall be alert - for many strange things shall come about in the time which is near ---

And I say unto thee which do read these words: Be ye not opinionated - for thy opinions shall be as the dew before the noon day sun -- Blest are they which turn unto their Source of being for all knowledge - for they shall come to know even as I know - and I have received my inheritance in full ---

I am a Son of God the Father - known within the Inner Temple as the Ancient of Days - called the Worthy Grand Master - Sanat Kumara

Sister Thedra of the Emerald Cross

Have I Not Sent Mine Emissary Out Before Me?

Sananda speaking:- Be ye blest of my being and of my presence - for I now come unto thee that ye may come unto me and that ye may know me as I know thee -- So be it in the name of the Most High Living God. So be it and Selah ---

Will ye not know me as I know thee? Have I not said that I shall give unto thee as ye are prepared to receive? And is it not the law? I say ye shall first prepare thyself to receive me-- And have I not sent my emissary out before me?- and have ye accepted her? Have ye given unto her credit for being that which she is?---

And have ye given unto her credit for being that which she is (this was repeated in the message) -- I say - as ye receive one of my emissaries ye have received me -- And too I say: As ye set foot against one of them ye have set foot against me - for I send my emissaries out in my name - and as ye are prepared to receive them - I send them unto thee ---

And as ye put thy hand to their mouth - so do you seal my lips -- And as I have said many times: When ye give unto one of my prophets the bitter cup - ye give it also unto me -- And when ye have gone the last mile ye shall know whereof I speak - such shall be thy knowledge.

I am now prepared to reveal many things unto thee which are prepared for such revelation ---

Now I am saying unto thee such things as shall profit thee to remember - and remember them ye shall - for it is now come when ye either go forward or move into another place -- For I say unto thee that the Earth shall no longer give unto the sleepers comfort - and she shall no longer mother an ungrateful civilization - an ungrateful people - for she shall vomit them out - and spew them up - for she is weary of them. And I say - the elements shall no longer obey the willful and wonton people which have thot themself wise -- Too I say that there are none so foolish as the one which thinks himself wise - and none so sad as he which betrays himself or his trust -- So be it that he shall be confronted with his foolishness - and he shall be brot to account for his foolishness. So be it and Selah ---

Now when I say I am within the secret place with many of my brothers from the realms of Light - I am speaking literally and truthfully for I am not a liar - and no man shall prove me a liar - for I am not to be found wanting ---

I have said I am within the Earth in a garment of flesh and bone - and I have come unto this one which now records these my words unto thee - and I have ordained her for this part as one qualified to speak unto thee for me - for I say she has been prepared for this part - and sent forth to do that which I have commanded of her -- So be it I say again: Woe unto anyone whosoever sets hand upon her -- And I say she shall be unto herself true - for I have sibored her wisely and I say the things she will not say --

So be it I shall speak that which I am of a mind to - and no man shall stay me or set his hand to my mouth -- And I am He which is Sent of the Father for the purpose of bringing thee out of darkness -- So be it, it shall profit thee to hear me out -- I have spoken - have ye heard me? I shall continue to speak and it shall profit thee to hear -- I am He which was born of Mary - and which was the ward of Joseph - once called Jesus of Nazareth - now known in this Temple as Sananda Son of God -- Amen - So be it and Selah

Sister Thedra of the Emerald Cross

The Places Held in Trust

Sanat Kumara speaking:-

Beloved of my being: Blest art thou and blest are they which come unto this altar in the name of the Father - Son and Holy Ghost --So be it and Selah ---

While it is still time I shall give unto thee this part which shall go out unto them which shall be prepared for the greater part -- And I say unto them that there are places within the Earth which has been prepared for this day and wherein man has not set foot -- Ye think thyself wise - yet ye know not that such places do exist - and let it go on record that these places are held in trust by the Hierarchy - and is the inheritance of them which are fortuned to be part of the new dispensation ---

This is the work of the new dispensation and it is given unto me - Sanat Kumara - to be the one responsible for this part of the work -- I have volunteered for this part - and I have given of my love and of my wisdom of myself - that this age may bear fruit -- So shall it - Amen and Selah ---

Blest are all which do accept that which has been held in trust for him -- I say unto him - he is no longer bound by the old law - he is under a new law - and he has been given a new dispensation whereby he may come into his inheritance in this day - and whereby he may have his legirons cut away ---

Now I say here for thy benefit - that there are none so foolish as he which thinks himself wise - and none so sad as he which betrays himself - or his trust ---

And it is given unto me to see thee seeking hither and yon for relief from all thy woes. Yet ye have not turned unto the source of thy being and ye have not asked of God the Father thy deliverance ---

I say unto thee in His name: When ye seek thy deliverance in Him and thru Him - He will send one of His emissaries unto thee and as ye receive him He shall send yet another - a Son of God -- And I say unto thee ye shall not be deceived - for there shall be given unto thee comprehension of these things ---

I say unto thee: Pray for comprehension and seek the Light of the Christ - and all that is necessary shall be revealed unto thee -- So be it and Selah ---

Now for the first time I speak unto thee on the subject:- Wherein I am are many which have come from other realms - from out thy Solar System have they come - and they are of the Father sent - even as I am sent ---

And with thy Lord and Master which ye have called Jesus of Nazareth - and which we call Sananda - sits one from out thy own system wherein there is only light - no darkness exists there -- And he has come that his Light may be added unto ours - and he is of great stature - for he stands fourteen feet tall by thy standards -- And we here in this temple know him as Bearea - for he has been unto thy solar system a Mentor and a Guardian -- We have asked of him that he may be unto us a lamp when thy Earth has seemed to go out of sight - for her blackness has been great -- She has had little light - and her darkness has been great indeed -- Be ye mindful of them which have gone out from their place of abode for thy sake ----

Now this brother Bearea - shall make himself known in the world of men - for he has great power within him -- For it is given unto him to be one with the Father that this may be accomplished in due time -- And when he speaks it shall profit thee to hear him - for he shall reveal great knowledge -- Such is his part ---

I am within this place wherein I am host unto him - and we herein sit at this council table for the good of all mankind -- And we are thy Benefactors which do guard and keep watch that thy Earth and the children thereof do not go into perdition -- Such is our mission - and it is thy part to hear that which we say unto thee - and to prepare thyself to receive the greater part - which is thy inheritance in full -- So be it and Selah ---

I am thy Benefactor and thy older Brother - Sanat Kumara

Sister Thedra of the Emerald Cross

SEAL OF SOLOMON

Sanat Kumara speaking: -

Blest art thou and blest are they which come unto this altar which the Father has set up -- So be it that many shall come thru these portals and I say unto thee: All which do come shall be blest - and so shall they come to know that which is willed unto them of God the

Father - and they shall receive of Him their inheritance -- So be it His Will - Amen and Selah ---

I am within the place wherein I sit in council for the good of them which shall be brot in - and blest shall they be - for they shall have upon their head a crown - and upon their forehead the Seal of Solomon ---

I say that in the time which is near many from among the populace shall be brot into the place wherein there is a Great White Altar of Alabaster - and they shall be fortuned that which has been held in trust for them ---

Now I say unto thee - ye shall be as one prepared - for none enter into this place unprepared - for it is the Father's Altar and none shall desecrate it -- I say we are not so foolish as to give unto fools our pearls without price -- We are not traitors nor do we give without the consent of the Father - for He has given unto us with wisdom and within the law -- And we abide by such law as He has fortuned unto us - we are not bound by it - for we are one with it - yet we transgress it <u>NOT</u> neither do we tempt the Father which has given unto us free will -- Such is wisdom ---

I say we are within this place as ones prepared for this day - and we have set up quarters within this place within the Great White Mountain wherein the White Altar of Alabaster now stands -- And with us is one from another solar system - which ye shall come to know - and ye shall be as ones given a great privilege to be blest of him and by him -- I am now prepared to give unto him the place of honor wherein he shall give unto thee his part and his blessings shall follow thee -- So be it and Selah ---

I am thy Brother and thy Sibor - Sanat Kumara

Sister Thedra of the Emerald Cross

There Is a Plan

Bearea speaking: -

Be ye blest of me and by me - for this do I reveal myself unto thee My beloved Sister of the Emerald Cross: It is only a short while since I last spoke unto thee in the high Andes - and at that time ye knew not that ye should return into thy home land for this part - and that I should come into the Earth for this my part -- I say it is the Will of the Father that we work within this place for a time - and that which is to be done shall be accomplished according to a great and divine Plan which has been brot forth from the Inner Temple - fashioned of the "ONE" and thru the love and mercy of our beloved Brother Sanat Kumara - known as the Most Worthy Grand Master - has this plan come forth -- I say the fullness of this plan shall be revealed unto them which shall be brot in. Such is the Father's Will -- So be it and Selah ---

Now I shall speak with thee on the morrow and I am glad -- So be it ye shall go from this altar in peace and with dignity - and I shall remember thee in the hours of thy sleep - Amen -- So be it in the name of the Most High Living God - and Selah ---

I am thy elder Brother - Bearea

Sister Thedra of the Emerald Cross

They Shall be Made Keepers of the Flame

Sananda speaking: -

Blest are they which come unto this altar and blest shall they be - for they shall come to know that which has been hidden from them ---

I say blest are they which keep their lights bright - and they shall be made Keepers of the Flame -- So be it that this day I shall speak with thee on the subject of <u>ONENESS</u> and for this do I come unto thee -- Be ye as one prepared to receive me and of me - and I shall give unto thee a part which ye shall give unto them which are yet in bondage ---

Now from the beginning of thy going out from the Father into the world of darkness have ye been one with Him in reality - yet ye have separated thyself from Him in thy own mind -- And in thy own UNKNOWING ye have forgotten thy identity and thy Oneness - for ye have not remembered Him - the Source of thy being - or the fortune willed unto thee of Him the Father -- And ye have been as ones soulless for ye have wandered as ones without direction - as ones lost in the wilderness - knowing not whither nor whence -- And ye have now reached a place wherein ye have no other place to turn -- Ye have no other way to go and ye have been as ones which have fortuned unto thyself all thy woes and torment ---

Ye have NO OTHER to blame - ye have NO OTHER to account to ye shall be either the victor or the loser ---

It is now come when great shall be thy woe - and so great shall be thy sorrow that ye shall fall upon thy face and cry aloud for mercy -- I say ye shall turn unto the Father - the Source of thy being for mercy - and ye shall put aside all thy pettiness and all thy puny ways - for it shall be unto thee thy own salvation ---

Now hear me in this: I say let no man cause thee to turn aside from thy appointed course -- Ye shall hold firm unto the course set before thee -- Ye shall be unto thyself true and give unto no man the bitter cup, for woe unto him which gives unto his brother the bitter cup ---

I am within the Earth for the purpose of bringing unto thee Light and I am not to be turned aside -- So be it and Selah ---

I am thy Sibor and thy Brother - Sananda

Sister Thedra of the Emerald Cross

The Ones Who Come That We be Lifted Up

Sanat Kumara speaking: -

Beloved of my being: Be ye blest of me and of my presence - for I now come unto thee that ye may be blest -- I now bring unto thee for them this part - which shall be given unto thee for them - and by thy grace shall ye receive it for them ---

Be ye prepared to receive the blessed and beloved from out thy own solar system which we know as Bearea -- And for this has he come that the way may be made clear that there might be free communication between this realm and thine -- I say there shall be ones prepared to receive him and of him - for he comes unto us as one qualified for his part which is given unto him of the Father of us all -- So be it and Selah.

I am one which has stood sponsor for thee - and I have sibored thee and wisely so -- Now ye shall record for them that which he has for them - and be ye as his hand made manifest unto them - so shall ye be blest -- Amen and Selah -- I am Sanat Kumara --

Bearea

Blest art thou among women - and blest shall ye be - for I come that ye be blest -- And I speak for the ones which now sit within this council chamber with me - that as ye come unto this altar which has been brot into manifestation - we thy Sibors and thy Brothers of Light - draw nigh unto thee - and we do breathe the breath of life upon thee -- I say we do breathe the breath of life upon thee - and as yet ye know not that which does sustain thee and hold thee fast ---

I say - we thy Sibors from the realms of light do hold thee fast in the hours of thy unknowing - and I say ye shall come to know us - for we have left our places of abode and come into thy place wherein ye labor for bread - that ye be delivered from bondage -- I say - we have gone out from our place of abode for thy benefit ---

For we have not gone into darkness for our own benefit - we need no such lessons - for we know wherein ye are bound - and by what ye are bound ---

And forever has it been: Wherein is darkness is no light - I say - wherein is darkness is no light -- And be ye as ones which have a will to turn unto the light and seek the Light of the Christ - and one shall come unto thee in the name of the Most High Living God - which shall be unto thee His hand made manifest unto thee - and He shall touch thee and ye shall be as one come alive -- And ye shall see him and know even as we see and know -- And ye shall drink from the Crystal Goblet the Living Water - and I say - all which drink of the Water of Life shall not die - for death shall have no power over them - and they shall be free - forever free as we - thy Sibors are free ---

I say unto thee we are not bound by any law - for we are one with all law - and we are true unto our station - we walk upright and with dignity -- We forget not our inheritance which is willed unto us of the Father which has given unto us being ---

Now for the first time I come into thy own Earth and I find herein many which are prepared to receive me and of me - and for this I am glad -- And from the beginning of my going out from my place of abode have I sent unto them my love and my wisdom and I have spoken unto them in the hours of their sleep - that they might be prepared to receive me - and of me ---

Let it be entered into this record that I have not spoken thru another. From the beginning have I prepared this Sister of the Emerald Cross for this part -- And too I say - I shall use no other channel -- Yet - let it be known that these fellow Brothers of Light do use many - and shall use any and all which are so prepared -- I say: Never within the history of man has it been so necessary that there be kindled within thy hearts the flame of Love - one for the other ---

I say ye shall pray without ceasing for love such as ye have not known - for the day draweth near when ye shall turn unto thy Source of being for Light and for Mercy -- And let it be said here: When ye do call out for mercy with thy heart black with hate - ye shall be as ones cast out - for I say ye shall be as ones cast out of thy own foulness ---

Blest are they which turn unto their Source and ask for light - and which do come clean of heart and hands ---

Such is my word unto thee - and I shall speak unto thee again and again -- Be ye at peace this day - and be ye poised - and I shall remember thee ---

I am thy older Brother and thy Sibor - Bearea

Sister Thedra of the Emerald Cross

The Gifts: Communication / Speech / Sight / Hearing

Bearea speaking: -

Blest are they which come to this altar - and blest shall they be for they shall come to know that which has been unto them their blessing.

I am come unto thee that they may come to know that which has hitherto been hidden from them - and ye shall be unto them my hand made manifest unto them -- And for this do I now give unto thee the authority and the power to speak in my name ---

And I say unto them as I would say - that when they have prepared themself they shall have the gift of communication and the gift of speech - the gift of hearing and the gift of sight -- For these are but parts of thy inheritance - and as yet they have but partial sight and hearing - and they use their gift of speech to defile themself and to desecrate the temples -- For they are blasphemous and they say not that which is prompted by love - and that which is given unto them of God the Father. They say that which binds them -- They are as ones bound by their own wonton - and by the darkness fortuned unto the unknowing ones -- Such is the pity ---

Now give unto them this word: When they use these gifts which are the lesser ones for the glory of God the Father - they shall be added in great measure and they shall see and know - even as we - thy Sibors see and know -- I say we see and know without limitation - for we are not bound by any limitation - We are free --

Blessed are they which are free - and I say we - thy Sibors have come from out the silence that ye may be free -- And I say unto thee: Forever clean thy heart of any and all hatred - all malice - and give unto the Father God all the glory and all the credit - and give unto thyself credit for being a Son of God -- And take unto thyself the responsibility of thy own self - and the part which has been given unto thee ---

Carry thy load with joy and thanksgiving - and call no man thy tormentor - for ye are alone responsible for all thy torment -- Ye alone are responsible!

Say unto thyself: He is not my salvation or my tormentor - he is my brother - unknowingly or knowingly -- I say ye shall take from him the power to torment thee ---

Ye shall be so filled with joy and love that he <u>SHALL</u> see thy light and thereby light the lamp ---

Such is my word unto them -- I say ye shall remember these my words - and when ye have learned them well - I shall give unto the greater things which ye have not dreamed of - and great shall be thy reward ---

I say - no man enters into the place of the Most High Living God unprepared - and I have come that ye may be prepared -- So be it it shall behoove thee to prepare thyself ---

And all the keys are contained within these my words - and have ye found them? Ye have but to seek within thy own temple for the light which never fails - and that which burns upon the Altar of the Most High Living God ---

Now within a short while one shall walk within the world of men as one fully qualified to give unto thee the Water of Life -- And I say ye shall drink thereof - and pass from thy dense form into thy Wholely Christ body - as one purified and as one cleansed from all darkness -- And death shall be no sting - for death shall have no power over thee - Ye shall ascend unto the Father - even as thy beloved Brother Sananda, the Lord and Master - which ye have known as Jesus the Christ -- I say within the record - that many have ascended - for this is the day when these things shall become common knowledge unto every man - and they shall know that which has been hidden from him -- Such is wisdom.

I say - revelation is a gift given unto thee of God the Father and willed unto thee as part of thy inheritance -- So be it ye shall prepare thyself for such revelation - such shall profit thee ---

I speak unto thee from out the secret place of the Temple of Light wherein sits the Council of many Lights - and I say they are within the Earth for the purpose of giving unto thee as ye are prepared to receive, no more - no less ---

Ye have been told and warned of such as shall come upon thee - and ye have not heard -- Ye have gone to sleep on thy feet -- And again and again the word has gone out from all the temples of Light: Prepare thyself for the Great Day is near - when the sun will give unto thee no light - and when ye shall be given much torment - or ye shall be removed into a place wherein is no danger or darkness -- I say ye have been warned - and yet ye sleep ---

I say: Yea - ye are as the walking dead - and ye shall be as ones which do seek the light - or ye shall go out in deep sleep -- And I say: Woe unto him which does go out in deep sleep - for he (these people) are the ones which have betrayed themself -- I say - there are none so sad as the one which betrays himself or his trust ---

Blest are they which turn their face homeward - for one shall be sent unto him and he shall receive that for which he has prepared himself ---

Keep ever before thee these my words - and I shall remember thee.

I am thy older Brother and thy Sibor -

Bearea - of the Sister Thedra of the Emerald Cross

They Shall Not Pilfer My Secrets

Sananda speaking: -

Beloved of my being: Blest art thou my beloved -- For this have I revealed myself unto thee - and ye shall come into the fullness of thy inheritance this day -- So be it the Father's will - and I am glad -- Amen and Selah ---

Ye shall give this unto them and they shall bear witness of these my words -- So shall it profit them ---

I say unto them - that they shall have proof of me - and I shall give unto the worthy proof -- Yet I shall not satisfy their curiosity nor shall they pilfer my secrets - nor shall I betray my trust -- For I am of the Father sent that His will be done in me - thru me - and by me -- And I do not betray myself or my trust - for I know the ones which are prepared to receive me and of me ---

I am not so foolish as to sibor fools - or give unto babes my pearls without price -- Too I say - that there are ones which have slept overtime and they shall be caused to awaken - and they shall be as ones come alive - and they shall arise and come forth - and they shall be glad their sleep has ended - for they shall be as one's awakened from a long and troubled sleep - wherein they have dreamed dreams which have tormented them ---

I am glad this day is come - for I say unto thee: There are many which shall come forth from out the populace which shall be unveiled and they shall stand forth in all their glory - for they shall be as ones which have the Crown of the Sun upon their heads - and the Seal of Solomon upon their forehead ---

I say that they now walk among thee unknown and uncrowned -- Yet I say they shall be unveiled - and they shall become known in the world of men - even as they are known unto us -- I say - be ye alert - for ye shall walk with angels unaware -- For this do I now speak unto thee - that ye may look for thy own light which burns upon thy own altar - within the Temple of the Most High Living God - and then ye shall see and know that which is now hidden from thee ---

First ye shall be true unto thy own self and unto no man give the bitter cup -- Such is wisdom ---

Now I say unto thee: Ye shall follow the law which is set down for thee and ye shall be blest -- For thy own sake do I remind thee of thy shortcomings - and I know thy weakness - and too - I know wherein thy strength lies -- Such is my knowing ---

I say unto thee: I am He which ye have called thy Brother Jesus of Nazareth - born of Mary and the ward of Joseph - now known within the place wherein I am as Sananda Son of God -- So be it - So let it be. Amen and Selah -- I have spoken unto my hand made manifest unto thee - known within this place wherein I am as Sister Thedra of the

Emerald Cross -- So be it she shall be blest of me and by me - and as I have willed it - So be it -- So be it -- Amen and Selah ---

Sister Thedra of the Emerald Cross

I Shall Instruct Thee in the Procedure

Sananda speaking:

Beloved of my being: Blest art thou and blest shall ye be - for I am now come that ye may be blest - for none shall place before thee a stumbling block - and none shall set his hand unto thy mouth ---

Now let it be said that there shall be one which shall come unto thee from out of the place wherein I am - and he shall instruct thee in the procedure which ye shall follow -- And this has been given unto the one which shall come from the Great Council of the White Star - or The White Brotherhood - as ye so frequently put it - it is lawful to speak thusly ---

Now ye have asked of us help of a practical type - and of that which shall be unto thee practical within thy own realms -- Such is lawful - for there is no need to give unto them which are not prepared to receive that which should choke them -- I say - we give not the babe at the breast the flesh of animals - such is wisdom -- I say - when they have come to the age of responsibility they shall be given accordingly - such is wisdom ---

Now was it not said in the beginning that one should come unto thee? And I say again - one shall come unto thee from out the place wherein I am - and he shall counsel thee and he shall give unto thee instructions in the way in which ye shall proceed within this temple -- And he shall be unto thee great light - and he shall be as none other - for he has been within this place for many moons - and he has not gone out ---

And I say unto them: Be ye not opinionated for ye shall be found wanting -- And there is none so foolish as he which thinks himself wise. So be it and Selah ---

I am with thee and I am glad -- Such is my part - to come unto thee that this plan may be fulfilled -- And so shall it ---

I am thy Sibor and thy Brother – Sananda

Sister Thedra of the Emerald Cross

I Come as a Forerunner

Bearea speaking: -

Blest art thou among women and blest shall ye be -- I am come that ye may be blest -- So be it in the name of the Most High Living God -- Amen and Selah ---

By my own hand shall ye be blest - for I say unto thee: I have come into the Earth from a far and distant galaxy that this age might bear fruit of a new kind -- And within the time which is near - nearer than ye can imagine - one shall be born of woman - from the womb of woman shall he be born and he shall come into the world of men as one sent of God the Father - and he shall be from out the realm which I call my own -- I come as the forerunner - I come that the world may be prepared to receive him ---

Now let this be recorded for them that they have not seen or heard of this one which shall come - for he has not been born of woman -- He is of the Father sent that this age may bear fruit of a new kind -- I say he is leaving his place of abode for the first time -- He has as yet not come unto the Earth as man - nor has he taken a body of flesh upon any other planet within thy own solar system -- For the first he shall be embodied within the world - and never at any time has he been born of woman ---

So be it that this shall be for the first time - and I say: Ye shall be within the body of flesh when he is born of woman - of the woman shall he be born ---

Give unto them these my words and say unto them as I would say that they shall put within the records these words which bear witness of these things which are yet to come -- And by thy hand shall these words be recorded for them -- And blest shall ye be - for ye know not that which ye shall do -- And I say ye have yet not begun the greater part ---

Give unto them this word - and they shall remember them -- At the age of twelve years - this one shall make his entrance within the world of men - and then I say unto them - he shall set up a temple upon a hill and he shall call forth the Maxin Light and it shall burn upon the top of this temple which shall be seen far and wide -- It shall beckon them from afar - and they shall come unto this temple of which I speak -

which shall be builded upon the hill - and therein they shall be prepared for their ascension ---

And I say - they shall no longer be the ones which die and rot within their graves -- They shall transmute all the elements of earthly substance - and take them with them into the realms of light from whence they came ---

They shall speak the "Word" and the elements shall obey their command -- And they shall be thy hand maidens in joy - and in thanksgiving -- They shall be unto thee that which ye will -- Such is my word unto thee ---

I have spoken unto thee from out the secret place wherein sit the Council of Light - that they may come to some knowledge of these things - So shall it profit them -- Amen and Selah ---

I am thy Sibor and thy older brother from yet another solar system. Bearea

Sister Thedra of the Emerald Cross

The Law is Swift Indeed

Sanat Kumara speaking: -

Be ye blest of me and by me - for I am come that ye be blest -- I say unto thee - ye shall be blest of me and of this Council -- Ye shall be blest of all which do sit with me - for within the place wherein I am are many which have come from out the realms of light that ye may be blest -- Have I not said that there is one among us at this time which is from a distant galaxy wherein there is no darkness - and if it were not so I would not tell thee ---

Now he shall speak with thee and ye shall give it unto them which are of this temple - and blest shall they be ---

I say: Not one shall misuse his words nor shall they say they are NOT SO - for I say unto them: Woe unto any man which desecrates them - for this one is sent even as I am sent of the Father -- And I say: The Law is swift indeed - and it shall rebound upon them -- I say - there are none so foolish as he which betrays himself -- And one which has within his mouth profanity shall surely reap the results thereof ---

Blest art thou that he has come unto thee -- I say ye have prepared thyself for to receive him and of him ---

Bearea

Be ye as one which has my hand upon thee and I shall bless thee O my child -- And be ye so blest of me that ye may be unto them that which I am unto thee -- I say: Ye have been blest so ye may bless others in turn -- Go into all the lands of the Earth and bless them ---

I say it is near when ye shall go out - and ye shall go into the land of Egypt and into the dark continent of Africa - wherein there is much torment - wherein there is no peace - and ye shall give unto them that for which they have waited -- They have waited such light as ye shall carry -- Ye shall then go out as one free from all bondage - free forever.

I say ye shall have free concourse into all the lands of the Earth and into all the nations of the Earth -- I say ye shall be unto them great light and much strength -- Ye shall counsel the heads of such governments as shall reign supreme -- I say that the heads of all the governments shall ask for thy counsel - for they shall be as ones bewildered and confused - and they shall be glad for thy light ---

I say ye shall go unto them in the name of the Most High Living God as one prepared and as one sent as an emissary of God the Father, I say the Father God has so willed it - and none shall deny Him nor shall they take away from Him -- He shall bring about the fullness of this plan which has been brot forth for the good of all mankind -- So be it and Selah ---

I have spoken unto thee my recorder - and ye shall give it unto them in my name and they shall bear witness of me - and that which I have said unto thee - for they shall come to know such things and it shall profit them ---

It is said that there shall be many brot out from the populace and they shall be prepared that they too shall go out for the good of all mankind -- I say that there shall be brot into this council chamber ones which are so prepared - and they shall be so instructed that they may serve in this plan in such capacity - and blest shall they be - for their reward shall be great indeed ---

I have spoken that they too may know that which goes on within the realms of light -- Amen -- So be it ---

I bless thee with my being - and with thy hand have ye recorded my words unto thee -- And ye shall sign thyself unto this document and unto all documents - for they shall go on record - and they shall become part of the permanent records now kept at Lake Titicaca -- Such is my word with and unto thee this day ---

I am thy Brother and thy Sibor - Bearea

Sister Thedra of the Emerald Cross

Forewarning

Sanat Kumara speaking: -

Beloved Ones: I say unto thee this day: One shall come unto thee and he shall be unto thee as one which has my hand upon him -- He shall be as one which has gone out from the place wherein I am - and he shall be blest of me and by me - and he shall be as one which has upon his head a crown - and upon his forehead a star ---

I say unto thee: He shall come unto thee as one prepared for that which shall be given unto him to do - I say he shall come as one prepared ---

Now ye shall prepare thyself to receive him and ye shall be as ones which have thyself in order - for I say he cometh in the name of the Most High Living God -- So be it ye shall receive him in such manner as is befitting a Brother ---

I am with thee and I shall bless thee -- So be it and Selah

I am Sanat Kumara

Sister Thedra of the Emerald Cross

The White Altar of Alabaster

Sanat Kumara speaking unto thee - that they may know that which is now established – I say unto thee that they may know these things which shall be revealed unto thee ---

Now when ye have been prepared for this part - ye shall be taken into the heart of this Mountain wherein stands the White Altar of Alabaster ---

And I say unto thee - ye shall say unto them as I would say - that there are none so foolish as the one which thinks himself wise - and none so sad as the one which betrays himself or his trust ---

When there is sufficient light within the - ye shall be brot into this place wherein there sits the Council of Seven Lights - and I say unto thee: The Council is now in session -- I say the Council sits within the place wherein the Altar of White Alabaster now stands - and on that Altar now lays the words which were written at thy fireside on the night of July - when ye did stand upon this Holy Ground -- I say - the words which were written now lay upon this Altar - and whereupon sits the Sananda -Sanat Kumara Symbol - which shall be read as follows: for first shall I give it unto thee .... This Symbol is not to be given out as such - for it is not to be made known unto the world of men ---

I say: Ye shall read this unto them - and they shall be as one which shall ask to see it - yet ye shall guard it for the future work -- It shall be unto them their proof - and none shall pilfer it - this Symbol ---

I am thy Sibor and thy Brother - Sanat Kumara

The Seal & Ring

Sanat Kumara speaking: -

Blest of my being: Blest art thou among women and blest shall ye be -- So be it and Selah -- I say unto thee: Ye shall be blest - for I now stand ready to come unto thee and to give unto thee that for which ye have waited -- Such is my part with thee - and I say I am not bound by the flesh as thou art ---

Now ye shall have upon thy forehead a Seal - and upon thy hand a shining Ring which is not of this world - for I say - ye shall go out from the place wherein ye are as one prepared -- So be it and Selah ---

Blest art thy partner for he has given unto thee richness of heart unknowingly -- I say he has served thee well - while not knowing ---

Now will it so that ye may be brot out ---

I am thy Sibor and thy Brother - Sanat Kumara

Sister Thedra of the Emerald Cross

The Poseid's Blessing

Sanat Kumara speaking: -

Beloved of my being: Be ye blest of me and of my presence - for this have I come -- I say unto thee - ye shall now receive that for which ye have waited -- Be ye blest of the presence of one which we know as The Poseid - and be ye as one which has his hand upon thee - and he shall bless thee and give unto thee that which shall prepare thee for thy part.

I say ye shall now record that which he has for thee - and it shall be for the good of all mankind -- So be it and Selah -- I am with thee and I shall stand sponsor for thee -- I AM - and I AM - for thy sake I am come unto thee that they may receive this - and for their sake do ye receive it for them which are of a mind to receive the greater part -- Amen and Selah ---

The Poseid

The Poseid speaking: Blest are they which receive me and of me - for I now come unto thee as one prepared - that ye may give unto them as ye do receive of us from out the realms of Light -- I say ye shall receive of us - and as ye do receive ye shall likewise do unto them which are so prepared -- I say as they are prepared so shall they receive - and so let it be ---

I say unto them - that when they have sufficiently cleansed their dwelling place - that they shall receive yet another wherein they shall dwell - within the realms of light wherein is no darkness -- And for this have we - thy Sibors which are not of the Earth and which are no part of darkness - come unto thee that ye may be delivered out ---

I say: When ye have delivered thyself out - and when ye have come out from among them which are yet in bondage - and them which do serve the dragon - one shall come unto thee and give unto thee as ye are prepared to receive ---

Such is our part -- I say we are of the Father sent - and we give not our pearls of price to babes which know not their worth ---

I say we do know their worth - and we do sibor thee wisely and we do come when ye are ready to receive of us - and by us -- It has been said many times: One shall come unto thee bearing a gift more precious than frankincense and myrrh - and so shall it be --

I say again - it is with the greatest of love and mercy that this one shall come - when ye are prepared to receive him----

He shall bear upon his forehead the Crown of the Sun -- He shall have within his hand a Crystal Goblet - beautiful beyond compare - and he shall have within the Goblet the Water of Life - from which all things perfect are made - and which makes perfect all which it touches ---

I say it purifies and cleanses all which it touches - and anyone which-so-ever drinks of this Liquid of Life shall not die -- They shall step forth from their body of earthly substance into their body of light substance as one delivered from all bondage - and from all darkness --

And their legirons shall be cut away - forever free shall he be -- So be it that their deliverance shall be unto them their Crown and their Robe of Light - The Seamless Garment -- And it shall enfold many which ye shall deliver up -- So be it and Selah ---

Now I say unto thee "---" - while it is yet time ye shall be as ones true unto thyself and prepare thyself - for ye shall be called in the midnight hour -- And ye shall hear that call and ye shall answer it and ye shall be glad indeed - when ye are prepared to receive the Cup Bearer. I say ye shall be glad indeed -- Such is my word unto thee ---

I am thy older brother and thy Benefactor - The Poseid

Sister Thedra of the Emerald Cross

(Legirons - Karma)

So Speaks the Grand Worthy Master

Sanat Kumara speaking unto thee: I say ye have gathered thyself into this temple for the purpose of learning the greater things -- I say as ye are prepared so shall ye receive ---

Now again I say unto thee: Ye shall be given as ye are prepared - and I have said that none enter into this place wherein I am unprepared. And too I say that when one is so prepared that he has done well and such is wisdom -- I say that none shall come into this place save thru the open door -- And too I say: I am the Grand Worthy Master - and I am Guardian of the secrets which are held in trust for them which are found worthy - and which do abide by such laws as is given unto the initiate upon the path - or the candidate for such initiations as shall make him eligible to enter into this temple --

I say - when he has properly prepared himself one shall come unto him and say unto him: My child So I have watched thy goings and thy comings - and I find thee worthy that ye may now be received into the place wherein I am going -- Ye shall now pass this way - and I say unto thee that which is wise and prudent -- Yet ye shall NOT be sufficiently learned to pass these portals by saying that which I have said unto thee for I am not so foolish as to give my pearls unto babes who know not their worth.

I say ye shall earn thy passport into all the secret places of the Earth And too I say - by thy works ye shall be known - and all thy good words shall avail thee nothing lest thy motives shall be clean -- Pure of heart and clean of hand shall ye present thyself -- I say again: All thy words of sweetness shall avail thee nought - when ye have within thy heart one iota of selfishness- and one dark place within thy heart ---

I say: Cleanse thy own heart and come clean of heart and hand - and one shall come unto thee and he shall lead thee out - and I shall meet thee at the door wherein I am - and I shall ask of thee three questions - and when ye can answer these truthfully ye may enter - and until then ye shall remain outside - while ye shall be as one in darkness and know not the workings of the temple ---

Now I say unto thee: Inasmuch as ye are faithful in little things - ye shall be made keeper of greater -- I say ye shall be given in greater capacity and in abundance -- I say - all law shall be revealed unto the just and the prudent which do enter into this temple wherein sit the Council of Seven Lights --

I say we are the Lights of this Temple -- I say we are the Guardians of thy Earth and the welfare thereof -- I say ye shall come to know of this Council and the workings thereof -- I say ye which are prepared to enter herein shall be schooled in the ways of the wise - and therein is wisdom -- So be it part of thy inheritance -- So be it the Will of the Father ---

I have spoken - so let it be as I have spoken -- And I have come unto thee that they may know that which I have said -- Such are my words - and give them unto them which are prepared to receive them - for none other shall receive them - such is their misery -- They are deaf and blind and I am not of a mind to give unto them sight and hearing until they ask that it be given unto them -- When they will it so - so be it - and it shall be as they will ---

I am he which guards this temple door - I am Sanat Kumara

Sister Thedra

Blest is He Which Serves with a Glad Heart

Sanat Kumara speaking unto thee at this altar this day -- Beloved ones: I say that none are excluded from this temple - yet not all are prepared for this part -- And when they shall find their way - and were it not so there would be no need for this my part of 'this plan'---

Be ye as one on whose shoulders rest great responsibility - for within the time which is near one shall come unto thee and he shall be unto thee thy hand maiden - he shall serve within the temple as one humble of heart and swift of foot ---

I say he shall serve in humbleness of heart and with joy -- So great shall be his joy that his feet shall be swift - and his hands shall serve in gratitude for his being ---

Blest are they which serve with a glad heart -- I am of a mind to bring him in and I shall be unto him great light - for he has served well within the place wherein I am -- And I say he is not one to betray himself or his trust - I say he shall serve in gratitude for his being - he shall not betray himself or his trust ---

Forget not that I have said he shall be as none other -- He has not been with thee in this place nor has he been in any other temple which has come into the outer manifestation -- He has gone out for the first time in many moons -- I say he has been within the place wherein I am for the purpose which he shall now serve -- I say for this part is he prepared for this have I prepared him ---

Now ye shall know him - for I shall give unto thee a sign and ye shall not be deceived -- So shall ye receive him into thy place of abode as a brother - and ye shall be glad for his coming -- So be it and Selah.

I am going to place within thy hand a packet wherein there shall be a sign - and that sign shall be his - and when he comes ye shall recognize it and ye shall be unto him a sister and he unto thee a brother And ye shall have no cause for tears -- Blest are they which are sent unto thee in my name --

I am sent of the Father - and I come unto thee in His name and for 'their' sake do I come that they may become even as He - the Father -- For He has given unto them free will - and when they choose to return unto their rightful estate willed unto them of God the Father - He shall send one out to show the way - to bring them out of bondage - out of darkness wherein they have been bound ---

I say: The day is now come when they which are so prepared shall be as ones which have upon their head the Corona of the Sun - and upon their forehead the Seal of Solomon -- I say - these shall step forth as the Sons of God revealed -- They shall not die - neither shall they taste of death - for death shall have no power over him -- Blest is he which is lifted up in the name of the Father - Son and Holy Ghost -- Amen and Selah ---

I am with thee unto the end -- I am Sanat Kumara

Sister Thedra of the Emerald Cross

Ye Shall Give Him Shelter

Sanat Kumara speaking:

I say unto thee my own - as I have not said before: I now stand ready to bring unto thee one which stands with thee - which shall be unto thee thy Shield and thy Buckler - and I say unto thee: Ye shall be as one which has my hand upon thee - and I say ye shall be as one which has given of thyself that they may be blest --

Now ye shall give shelter unto he which is to come - and he which shall be unto thee a hand and a foot -- And I shall be unto him all that is necessary - for he shall come unto thee as a brother - and he shall be as one which has a mind to serve the Christ -- And he shall be as one sent of God the Father - and he shall stand by thee as one which has the will to serve the Light ---

I say: He shall serve the Light with all his strength - and I say - ye shall have cause for rejoicing -- So let it be - Amen and Selah ---

I am now prepared to bring him unto thee -- So be it that he is now prepared - and I am glad -- So be it ye shall receive him in the name of the Father - Son and Holy Ghost -- Amen and Selah ---

I am Sanat Kumara

Sister Thedra of the Emerald Cross

Responsibility of This Altar

Sanat Kumara speaking: -

Beloved of my being: Blest art thou and blest shall ye be -- And now ye shall be as one which has my hand upon thee and ye shall be blest even as I am blest ---

Be ye as one prepared to receive him which shall come unto thee and ye shall be blest of him and by him ---

I am within this place wherein I am as one prepared to send him - and for this is he prepared -- And from this day forth shall ye be as one on whose shoulders rests the <u>responsibility of this altar</u> which has been set up within the outer place - and in the name of the Most High Living God -- So be it thy responsibility shall be great indeed - and I am with thee unto the end ---

Now ye shall be as one which has the part of "---" - and he shall have that of the "---" -- And again I say that thy younger sister shall have the part of altar service -- She shall attend the altar and prepare the service - It shall be as that of no other - for it shall contain a basin of fresh clean water - and it shall be as one which has cleansed the hands -- And there shall be a glass and that glass shall contain fresh clean water --

And each sip from it in remembrance of me -- And I say I am of the Father sent that ye may drink of the goblet of life - and I say ye each shall drink from the goblet - first thyself - second unto thy right. And it shall pass from hand to hand until it is returned unto Wanica - which shall partake of the last drop and return it unto the altar ---

I say the altar shall have upon it the linen which is new - virgin linen, and used for nothing else - I say it shall be for the altar only --

Now ye shall come unto this altar in silence -- And too I say - ye shall be as one in authority - and when one among thee finds fault with this procedure he shall be excluded -- I say I am of the mind to cast them out -- And they shall not come unto this altar with criticism upon their lips - or for the purpose of giving unto themselves credit for being wise ---

I say that I am the Master within this temple - and I know that which I say and do -- And I am not of a mind to give unto the foolish my pearls without price -- I command of thee obedience in all things -- I give unto thee a commandment this day: Be ye as one prepared to receive him which shall come unto thee and he shall come as one sent of God the Father ---

I say he shall come unto thee for the purpose of serving the plan -- He shall serve with all his strength -- So be it and Selah ---

I am with thee and I shall not forsake thee ---

I am thy Brother and thy Sibor - Sanat Kumara

Sister Thedra of the Emerald Cross

Such is a Fool Indeed

Sanat Kumara speaking unto thee - which is my hand made manifest unto them: I say that they shall hear me - and they shall comprehend that which I say unto thee -- For it is now come when ye shall be brot out from the places wherein ye are - and ye shall find therein no hiding place -- And ye shall be as ones with no place to lay thy head - for within the time which is near-ye shall be as the foxes and ye shall be as ones which have thrown overboard thy own life belt --

For I say unto thee: Ye have been told many times that the day of sorrow is nigh upon thee and yet ye are deep in lethargy - and ye have not stirred within thy tracks - ye have been as ones with feet of lead - ye have moved as with leaden feet -- Ye have been slothful in thy ways and ye have been as ones which have upon thy back the burden of the ass - and ye have been as the tillers of the soil which know not the seasons ---

Ye have sown in the fallow places nought - ye have sown in the fertile places nought -- Ye have sown upon the rocks - ye have given unto the winds the power to scatter thy grain and ye have squandered thy fortune - and ye have been found wanting ---

I say ye have squandered thy substance - and I say ye have given of thy substance unto the thieves who would rob thee and who would call thee fools ---

I say ye have given unto the thieves that which has made of thee paupers - and ye have been as the foolish virgins -- I say ye are now out of oil -- I say ye have squandered thy substance such is a fool indeed.

I am not so foolish - for I am now prepared to bring them out from among thee which are prepared for this part - which shall be revealed unto the <u>just</u> and the prudent -- And I say unto them: Be alert and ye shall bear witness of me - and ye shall have upon thy head the Crown of the Sun and the Seal of Solomon shall be upon thy forehead -- So be it and Selah ---

I am not so foolish as to waste my substance - for I am of the Father sent that ye may be brot out of bondage - and that ye may have light abundantly -- I say that ye shall have light abundantly which are so minded to follow me - for I shall lead thee into the place wherein I shall reveal many things unto thee which are prepared for such revelation.

I am he which is responsible for this new dispensation - for I have brot it forth from out the Inner Temple wherein the Father is -- So be it I am he which is known as the Most Worthy Grand Master -- So be it - Amen and Selah ---

I am thy Sibor and thy older Brother - Sanat Kumara

Sister Thedra of the Emerald Cross

Small Parts Make up the Whole

Sanat Kumara speaking: -

Be ye blest of my presence - for I am come that ye may be blest -- And I say unto thee: This house shall be blest this night - for one has come into it who shall be as one on whose brow shall rest the symbol of Peace - I say - on his brow shall rest the symbol of Peace - and that peace shall be unto him his Shield and his Buckler ---

I say he shall be blest for the presence which is and which he shall come to recognize -- I say by my presence shall he be blest --

So be it he shall come to know me - and he shall come to know that which shall be unto him his passport into the secret places of my abode. For I say - he shall pass within these portals as one which knows and he shall know that he knows - and such is wisdom --So be it and Selah.-

I am now prepared to give unto him a part which shall be unto him great wisdom - great shall be his light -- So be it and Selah ---

Now say unto him as I would say - that he shall bring forth one from out the south wherein he shall go - which shall be unto me my hand made manifest unto them - and he shall be as one which has gone into the southland as for to bring back this one ---

I say that the one which has the fortune to be unto him his <u>mate</u> shall be unto them my hand made manifest unto the ones which have a mind to learn -- And he shall be as one which shall be unto her her hand maiden ---

She shall do that which shall be commanded of her - and he shall be unto her that which shall be commanded of him -- And they shall work as a team -- Such is wisdom ---

I say unto him - he has found his way into this place as part of the plan -- So be it and Selah ---

I am thy older Brother - Sanat Kumara

Sister Thedra of the Emerald Cross

Remember the Ones Which Have Prepared the Way

Sanat Kumara speaking: -

Beloved of my being: I am come that ye may be blest this day -- And I say unto thee ye shall be blest - for one shall come unto thee which has my hand upon him - and he shall be unto thee thy hand and thy feet -- And he shall be as none other has been - he shall be as one on whose shoulders shall rest the responsibility of thy welfare ---

I say he shall take upon him the responsibility of thy welfare and he shall be unto thee that for which he is sent -- I say he is sent of God the Father that this plan may be brot forth -- Such is the plan for him - and he shall not fail thee - nor shall he betray himself or his trust ---

I am now prepared to bring him unto thee and ye shall be glad -- So be it and Selah -- I am with thee unto the end ---

Now ye shall say unto the one which has within his hand that which shall be given unto him - that he shall go in peace - and I shall direct him and he shall follow the directions which I shall give unto him ---

He shall go straitway and not tarry for nought -- He shall return immediately - and when he arrives at his destination in the north I shall speak unto the one which shall be my hand made manifest and I shall put into her mouth the words which shall be unto him the words of wisdom ---

I say: Thru her I shall direct him - yet he shall not forget from whence his blessings -- I say he shall remember the ones which have prepared the way before him -- I say I shall direct him - yet he shall be mindful at all times of his blessings - he shall give unto the Father credit for his being - and unto his Benefactors credit for his well being ---

I am within the place wherein I am prepared to reveal many things unto him - and I say - he shall be as one alert and mindful of all his blessings and the Source thereof -- So shall it profit him ---

I am thy Sibor and I have spoken -- So be it - and be it so ---

I am Sanat Kumara

Sister Thedra of the Emerald Cross

Mission Statement

Give the truth to the world. Let it be received where it will. Many will read the messages. Some will accept the truth, others will read through curiosity, a few will ridicule. Yet to all is the truth given, and to all remains the power of choice.

The hope of the world in these times is in spiritualizing all forms of activity---promoting understanding through love and service. These must be the watchwords if the world is to come into lasting peace. We are trying to influence a world that is going astray and could cause undreamed of suffering. We are trying to overcome the thought of materialists and to bring a spiritual outlook into the earthly life. We need the help of all on earth who can think in spiritual terms. The great battle to be fought now is between the spiritual and the material, between idealism and carnalism. You can help by spreading the word---we are asking that you help because the battle may be long and the victory far away.

Halls of Light is not allied with any sect, denomination, political entity, organization, neither endorses nor opposes any cause. There are no dues for membership. Halls of Light is self-supporting through its own voluntary contributions. Halls of Light has but one purpose: to help through encouragement and understanding...

To contact the publishers or to obtain copies of our other books, please contact us at email: goldtown11@gmail.com

Sananda's Appearance

Be ye as one which hast heard Mine Voice and responded unto it - for I speak that ye hear, and I say that which is wise and prudent.

Let it be known that 1, the Lord thy God hast spoken and bear ye witness of Me, for I have made manifest Mineself that ye might know Me - and for this wast these manifestations made.

I say that I have made Mineself manifest that ye might see Me with thine mortal eyes; that ye might bear witness of Me. Yet thine companions saw and believed not; neither did they hear, for they were selfish and unprepared - yet, did I deny them?

I say; I came that they which would might see and hear. I went and came again unto Mine own. So be it that I have found; I have given unto the found that they which know not might know; that they might come to know as thou knowest.

Yet, how many hast turned from Me and persecuted thee for Mine Word. It is said, "Woe unto them which persecute Mine servants." is it not the law which they set into motion?

Yea Mine beloved, I say they bring about their own downfall. So be it that I am a compassionate one, and I would that they know what they do. So be it they shall learn well their lessons. So let it be, for this is the mercy of God, the One which hast sent Me.

So be it. I AM The Wayshower, the Lord thy God

I AM Sananda

About the Late Sister Thedra

Since the later part of the last Century, the *Kumara* wisdom has begun to reemerge into the world. This process began with the late Sister Thedra, whom Jesus Christ appeared physically to while on her deathbed and spontaneously healed her of cancer while she was in the Yucatan, where she had gone to accept her fate and the will of our Lord Jesus Christ.

That is when something miraculous occurred. Jesus spoke to her saying, "My name is Esu Sananda Kumara" and then sent Thedra down to the Monastery of the Seven Rays in Peru to learn the Kumara wisdom. After five years, Thedra was told to return to the United States where she founded the Association of Sananda and Sanat Kumara at Mt. Shasta in California.

While heading this organization, Thedra channeled many messages from Sananda and taught the Kumara wisdom until her passing in 1992. While in the Yucatan, it is said that Sister Thedra, during the 1960s, was associated with the Kumara.

Sister Thedra, 1900-1992, spent five years at an abbey undergoing intensive spiritual training and initiations. While in South America, she had an experience which changed her in an instant when, as it is told by her, Jesus Christ physically appeared to her and spontaneously cured her of cancer.

He introduced himself to her by his true, name, "Sananda Kumara," thereby revealing his affiliation with the founders of the

Great Solar Brotherhoods. It was by His command that Sister Thedra went to Peru. She eventually left upon being told that her experience there was complete. She then traveled to Mt. Shasta in California and founded the Association of Sananda and Sanat Kumara. A.S.S.K.

You ask, Is There a difference between Jesus and Sananda? Our Lord's name given at birth by his Father Joseph and his beloved mother Mary was Yeshua, thus being of the house of David and the order of Yoseph he would be called Yeshua ben Yoseph. The Roman Emperors placed the name of Jesus upon the sir-name of Yeshua after the Emperor Justinian adopted Christianity as the official faith of Rome and ordered that the sacred books be compiled upon approval of a specially appointed counsel appointed by the Emperor into a recognizable and uniform work titled "The Bible". Prior to this, there never was a Bible per se.

There existed until the time of the Emperor's edict, a selection of many Sacred texts, that were employed in the Sacred Teachings, many of which were copies of what the Greeks had transposed from the original texts in the Libraries of Alexandria, which were originally compiled by Alexander the Great, and were destroyed by Julius Caesar who feared that they might prove dangerous to the rule of a Caesar, an Earthly God.

In addition, it was to keep the knowledge of Alexander's Libraries out of the hands of the Ptolemy's who were said to be descended from his bloodline. (At the time, Caesar had no way of knowing that vast portions of the Library were already in the

Americas, in the Great Universities of the Inca, and in possession of the Mayans.)

Yeshua spent many years in the East after his ascension. The Good Shepherd, upon his appearances to the Apostles after His ascension, told them that He was going to tend to His Father's other sheep; which meant, plainly, that He was continuing upon His sacred journey. As The Ascended One, Yeshua took to Himself the name of Sananda, meaning the Christed One, and Sananda was thus embraced forevermore by the Great Solar Brotherhood. To many of you. this is all new. To others it will be received as a welcome easing of the wall that has so long separated two sides of the same coin. This knowledge is being placed into the ethers and the matrix of thought at this time as it is the time of The Great Awakening and the Christos is already emerging into the new consciousness.

Authority to use the name of Sananda was given to Sister Thedra when Jesus, (Sananda) appeared to her in the Yucatan and cured her instantly of the cancer that had taken over her body. Further, He allowed a picture of his countenance (included herein) to be taken at that time that she might realize the occurrence was more than a dream.

Sanada's Message to her by Sister Thedra: "Sori Sori: Mine hand I have placed upon thine head, and I have given unto thee the authority to use Mine name. Give unto them the name Sananda, by which they shall know Me as the Lord thy God - the Son of God, sent that ye be made to know me, the One sent from out The Inner Temple that there be Light in the world of men. Now it is come when ones which have the will to follow Me shall come to know Me by that name which I commanded thee to give unto the world as Mine New name.

There are many that shall call upon the name of Jesus, yet they will deny the new name as they are want to do. Unto thee I give assurance that I am the One sent that there be Light in the world of men. Now let this be understood, that they that deny Mine New Name, deny Me by any name. So be it I have appointed thee Mine spokesman; I've given unto thee the power and authority to speak for being that which I AM. And I say unto thee Mine child whom I have called forth and anointed thee with the Holy Spirit, thy name shall be as it is now called, Thedra, that name I spoke unto thee from out the ethers, and thou heard Me and accepted that which I gave unto thee; and wherein have I deceived thee? Wherein have I forgotten thee, or left thee alone?"

I say unto thee: "Mine hand is upon thee and I shall sustain thee and you shall come to know that which I have kept for thee. So be it that I have kept thy reward, and at no time shall it be dissipated or scattered, for it is intact. So let this Mine Word suffice them which question thee - let them question, and I shall bear witness for thee. For do I not know Mine servants from the traitors? Do I not reward Mine servants according unto their works or merits? I speak that they might know that I am mindful of Mine servants, that I am not a poor puny priest who has forgotten his servants.

"I say unto them, Mine servants shall be glorified above the crowned heads of the nations which have set themselves apart, and denied Me Mine part of Mine word for they have turned from Me in their conceit and forgetfulness. Now let this go on record as Mine

Word, and I shall give unto them proof, which are of a mind to follow Me. So be it as I have spoken and I am not finished; I shall speak again and again, and I shall rise Mine Voice against them which set foot against Mine servants, and they shall be as ones cast out. So let them ask of Me and I shall enlighten them. So be it I know where of I speak. Be ye as ones blest to accept Me and know Me for that which I AM."

On Saturday, June 13, 1992, at exactly 10.00 PM, at the age of 92, Sister Thedra made her final transition from the comfort of her own bed. When the time arrived, she simply took one small breath and slipped quietly away, without pomp or fanfare.

She left as she had lived: as a humble servant for the greater good. The messages included were given to Sister Thedra before her transition. They are compiled here to give you some idea of the significance of her passing and of the expansion of the work, as she is now free to work unencumbered by the physical limitations and by the pain which has so encumbered her in the past. She has carried on the work here on the Earth plane for the last 50 years because that is where the work was needed. Rest assured that her work now in the higher realms will simply be an extension of that work.

Divine Explanations

Part - I

The following explanations and definitions of terms used by Sananda (Jesus) and the various Sibors were given by Sananda through direct revelation. They are not alphabetical. These explanations should be read over and over.

- - - - - - - - - - -

"My Beloved Sibors please give us plainly the definitions of the following words that there may be no error on our part." - Thedra.

THEMSELF? What is the explanation of your terminology of "Themself" – "themselves"?

"I (Sananda) say unto thee mine beloved, they which would be unto thee a vessel, unto thee a sibor, unto thee teacher, are as ones enlightened of the Father, enlightened of the Father for the light is in them.

They know their parts well, they have their memory, they have mastered the elements, they can do all the things which I do and they take unto "themself" no credit for they have overcome self. They are self-less. Now I say unto them: them which work with thee are the Selfless ones. They ask nothing for "themself." Now while this is true they are as one.

They are within the great brotherhood of the Selfless Ones - the Ones clothed in white. They are as the Royal Assembly - and each unto his own, yet each for all and all for one. Now while in thy world, they (of thy world) are <u>selfish</u> and they are not for the whole - they ask for self and I speak of these as the selfish ones. I speak unto them in terms which they shall come to know and therein is wisdom.

I say that they shall be responsible for "themself" and as a world of me I say they shall be responsible for their society; they "themself" have created it. Now I speak unto thee mine beloved, I say "ye shall be responsible for thyself. He shall be responsible for himself. They as a whole shall be responsible for that which they have created, while thou art responsible unto thyself for thine part - and not held accountable for theirs. Be it so."

BELEIS? "Mighty is the word and great the power thereof. I say unto thee this word carries with it the part of surrender. The word is the release of power - that which is sent forth by the one which asks of the Father His blessing. It is the surrender of the self - the complete surrender of the personal will and letting the Father's will be accomplished in all things through thee. "<u>So</u> <u>be</u> <u>it</u>" - it the accomplishment, the acceptance of the Father's plan."

SELAH? - "The word carries the Seal of Truth - meaning it is without error - no mistake - it is the verification of Truth - not subject to change.

SIBET? – "The Sibet is one which has offered or presented himself as a candidate for the greater learning and for the greater initiation. He comes as an empty vessel that he may be filled. So be it."

SIBOR? - "I am the Sibor of Sibors." - "The Sibor is one which has been illumined of God the Father. He has returned unto the Father purified. He has gone the Royal Road - which means he has overcome death. He has mastered the lower elements - he controls the elements. He can raise the dead - heal the sick - he can create like unto the Father <u>for</u> he has finished his course and won the victory and returned unto the Father the Victor. So be it."

"I am the Sibor of Sibors. I am the first born of Him which hast sent me. Sananda."

LEGIRONS? - "Beloved - I say unto thee: thy opinions and thy dogmas are not the least of these - neither thy creeds. Be it ever that these are great and heavy ones. Now let it be understood that a leg-iron is something which holds thee bound. It is something which holds thee, it keeps thee fast, wherein progress is not possible. Now that progress be made possible, ye shall cut away the legirons.

Knowest thou these bound by legirons? These are to be pitied, they drag them with them, impeding their progress - and they are as ones bound! They are not free - are they? While they serve their sentence - they are as ones bound - they are bond-men - they are bound men - men bound. Now let me say I too am a "bondsman." I came that they may be free. I say I bring unto thee the law which thou shall obey - unto the letter - then I shall give unto thee that which I have kept for thee. Be ye as one prepared for that.

PREPARATION? Now - preparation - what do you mean by "preparation?" "This my beloved is the part which they shall do - the part of preparation is: cleaning thyself of all the opinions, indoctrinations of man. The cup must be emptied. This is thy part, the becoming the '"little child" unopinionated, unscathed and unmarred with or by their doctrines, creeds and crafts. I say the child is unindoctrinated and un-opinonated and is the virgin mind – (yet it does not remain so long in this world). While the little child represents the empty cup - the empty vessel, the Virgin Spirit, it is given unto the child to be one which has come from other realms and to have been in many embodiments, many times: yet the symbol of virginity. Wherein is it said there are none innocent among thee?

WHEREIN I AM? - "Now while thou art yet within the world of men - I am within mine Father's realm, the place wherein there is no darkness, wherein <u>ALL</u> things are known. I say wherein <u>ALL</u> things are known, wherein there is <u>No</u> mystery.

And too - I say when thou hast attained unto thy Royal Road, when thou hast become part of the Royal Assembly, thou shall know as I - thou shall be as I - thou shall be brought into the place wherein I am, for I say unto thee this is attainment. This is the day of Attainment, the day of "becoming," the day of thy salvation. Know ye that this is Mine day - the day for which thou hast waited? I say unto thee: "This is the day of fulfillment. This is Mine Day. Mine Day is come ---"

What is meant by "ALL THE LANDS OF THE EARTH?"- "This I mean, all the lands of the Earth. I have said it, I mean it as I have said it and there is no mystery of or to it."

ALL MANKIND? "This is Mine people - Mine children - Mine flock - Mine Church - Mine brethren - Mine congregation unto whom I shall minister. By Mine own hand shall they be fed and led. These have I came to find. Are not all <u>hu</u>-man beings considered "Man kind"? by thine own standards. Yet all men are not of me."

WHAT DO YOU MEAN - "WILL IT SO"? - "There is power in the "WILL" and the power which they use to create their own torment and confusion is misused energy. Yet they will this - they will it so. Now when ye will to serve me ye give unto me thy undivided attention, the whole heart - thy heart - thine ALL. Yet I say that they which doth attempt to serve me with one hand and the dragon with the other has not willed to serve me. They are not of me - they are not of Mine flock. I say they are either with me or against me. I cannot accept the one hand while they reserve the other for the dragon. They are not wholeheartedly mine.

I make no compromises with the dragon. Mine shall come out from them and surrender unto me themself - their all - without reservation. This is willing it so - for they will the Father's will be done in them, through them, by them. They leave no energy that the dragon may use. They use all their energy to serve me. This is mine word unto thee."

WHAT IS DARKNESS? - "Thine Un-Knowing - thy darkness comes from the fall of man - which one was with God the Father perfect which didst have his memory blanked from him when he didst transgress."

MAYAS VEIL? - "The result of such unknowing - the darkness which man has brought upon himself. The part he has created for himself."

WHAT DOES IT MEAN TO <u>BETRAY</u> <u>ONES</u> <u>SELF</u>? - "This is the sad part for first the 'fall' came from his betrayal - and it hast resulted in the fall - in the veil of Maya - the "illusion" and in thy un-knowing - in thy own darkness."

WHAT OF BETRAYING "HIS OWN TRUST"? - "The plan is all inclusive and includes all - yet there are ones unaware of the "plan" - (and they are not as included in this temple as yet) - no personal reference unto the ones within this temple. Now when one becomes aware of his part, he is given the law and it is provided for his own good - and he has the law clearly stated, plainly recorded, and he turns his face away - that he may hide from it. He puts his fingers into his ears that he may not hear it. He gives unto his benefactors the bitter cup and he goes his own willful way.

He has betrayed himself for he shall be caught up short of his course. When he has been given a chance - a "part" within the plan and he has committed himself, he has the responsibility given unto him for that "part" and should he be so foolish as to betray his trust he shall be like unto one which has thrown overboard his own life belt - poor foolish ones!"

WISDOM? - What is meant by the word "Wisdom?" - "Wisdom is that which is light, the knowledge of the law and its proper use. The right use of the law - and this Mine children is Mine part. I come that ye may BECOME wise! Wisdom is thy divine gift - not of man, for man of Earth is foolish indeed - and he is nothing save that which the Father has endowed him. All else is of the world of "illusion" which shall pass into nothingness in the Light which I Am."

WHAT IS THE "PEARL OF GREAT PRICE, THE PRICELESS PEARL? - "That which I offer thee - thy freedom, thy salvation from bondage - thine inheritance in full - Mine word which is not purchased with coin - not bought, neither is it sold. It is the wisdom of which I speak. Mine offer unto thee is without price - it is the 'pearl' - "Mine Pearl."

WHY ARE MIS-SPELLED AND GRAMMATICAL ERRORS USED IN THESE SCRIPTS? - "I am not a conformist. I am not concerned with the letters of man for I am He which has come that they be unbound by their fetters. I say unto them which desireth the letter - unto them the letter.

I say unto thee: be ye as ones free from such bondage. I stand ready to free thee from thy bondage. Unto thee I say - give unto the letter no thought. <u>Hear</u> what I <u>say</u> for I shall say it in many ways as becomes me and serves mine purpose. I say I am no stranger in thine midst. While they know me not, I know them. I see them bowing down before the Golden Calf - and they worship at the shrines which they have set up. (Their own standards of education.) They guild them and bring unto them burnt offerings - yet they close me out.

Be ye not so foolish. <u>Be</u> <u>ye</u> <u>not</u> <u>so</u> <u>foolish</u>! I am come that ye might have Light - Wisdom - Freedom which is the Father's will. While the letter changeth and passeth away - and the letter is not the law - the letter is of no consequence other than to cause thee to see the "Word." The word is the power which shall provoke thine mind into action and thy mind shall be free from the letter. See what is meant within the Word, and let thine mind be staid on <u>me</u> - the Light, the Way - Truth and Wisdom."

"I am He which hast come - that ye be free: forever free. I am Sananda - Son of God. Once known as the Nazarine, He which was born of Mary, Ward of Joseph.

Recorded by Thedra

Part - 2

THE WHITE BROTHERHOOD AND THE EMERALD CROSS.

THE MANY QUESTIONS ABOUT THE WHITE BROTHERHOOD AND THE ORDER OF THE EMERALD CROSS MAY BE EXPLAINED IN A FEW SIMPLE WORDS.

ONE HAS TO EARN THE RIGHT TO BECOME A MEMBER - EITHER IN THIS LIFE OR OTHERS BEFORE OR AFTER - NONE ENTER UNPREPARED.

THE WHITE BROTHERHOOD - or - THE ROYAL ASSEMBLY is of the Realms of Light---not of Earth. The Ascended Masters have proven themself in the school of Earth (THE SCHOOL FOR GODS) who have trodden the path of INITIATION - overcome the trials and temptations of the mundane world - who have gained their freedom and ascended as the Lord Jesus Christ (Sananda). They have gone the ROYAL ROAD.

Knowing the path of the Initiate -- and its pitfalls -- and sorrow, they extend a hand in Fellowship - LOVE and WISDOM - NEVER depriving the candidate an opportunity to learn his lessons well -- for this is His salvation -- for this do they proffer their hand, NOT to do our part for us, but rather that we become strong and free by our own strength.

The Royal Assembly or the White Brotherhood have known all of the heartaches, the longing, crucifications, temptations and JOYS of the aspirant -- the candidate -- the Master -- the Sibor -- herein lies their strength, their understanding, their great love for us on the path.

Their love and understanding knows no bounds. They give help when necessary for our progress. They also withhold it wisely - should it deprive us of our lessons. The candidate on the path of initiation shall become self-responsible for all his actions -- all the energy allotted him throughout his whole EARTHLY existence - and make atonement for all his misused energy, for therein is his salvation.

There is no one else which will ever make this atonement for us (the candidate) on the path of unfoldment. While the host of "WHITE BROTHERS" Brothers of LIGHT are ready to assist, the candidate shall (MUST) put forth every effort to overcome all the forces of darkness which would deter his progress and earn for himself his freedom from BONDAGE.

THE EMERALD CROSS

THE EMERALD CROSS is a company – and an order of beings who work within the Brotherhood of MAN - and the Fatherhood of God - for the good of all mankind --- And at the head of this group is one known as MOTHER SARAH, the personification of love -- embodiment of all MOTHERS. That is: the LOVE of God made Manifest - in MOTHERS. The blessed Mother Sarah is the head of this Order of the Emerald Cross. And when one earns the Divine right and privileges to associate themselves with this Order, it is the joy of all the Orders - and Brothers of Light. I speak for the Order - for I am known as Merseda. (As told to Sister Thedra of the Order of the Emerald Cross).

COMANCHE - which is the porter at the door - which doth keep out the unworthy, the unjust, the unclean. The Door Keeper - the one responsible for the Temple Gate.

BITTER CUP - that which you would not like to partake of - that which poisons thee, that which is not good, that which torments thee - that which ye have given unto thy brother to torment him which returns unto thee as a boomerang to torment thee - which ye shall receive multiplied - which has accumulated in its swift flight. I say prepare not for thyself the bitter cup for ye shall drink of the portion which thou doth prepare for thy brother. Be ye not foolish - make it not bitter.

BLEST OF MINE BEING - I have given of Mine self that Mine beloved has being.

BLEST OF MINE PRESENCE - Have I not gone the long way? I have gone out from Mine place of abode that I might bring light unto the Earth that she might be lifted up - that the children thereof might be delivered of all bondage - that they might return unto the place from whence they went out. And have I not come unto thee many times that this be accomplished? Have I not done all which has been given unto me to do? Wherein have I failed thee? Have I not done all that I have come to do? - While it is not as yet finished, I shall not fail. My mission shall be finished ere I return unto Mine abiding place. Shall I not be unto the true and shall I not return the Victor?

GAVE OF HIMSELF - Did I not give of Mine Self - hast thou? Have I not been true unto Mine trust? Have I asked aught for Myself? Have I not done that which I have promised? Have I not given Mine All? Have I not come on a Sacrificial Mission? What more have I to give - other than myself?

PORE - The physical body - vehicle which thou dost use.

INITIATION - Thy preparation for the inner temple. Each step is an initiation. One step at a time - the overcoming of self - the world - the becoming that which I am.

COSMOS - That which is unseen throughout many universes by thy eyes. Great is the expanse of the Father's Kingdom and the total thereof is referred to as "throughout the Cosmos."

LORD'S STRANGE ACT - This I shall reveal in Mine own time.

WALK WHICH WAY THY CROWN TILTS NOT - as a Son of God. Do honor unto thy Father Mother God - and thou shall be as one which has the Royal Raiment upon thine shoulders - and ye shall wear it in honor and with dignity.

WHEN IT SAYS IT IS RECORDED - WHEREIN IS IT RECORDED? - In the secret place - in the eth - and within the inner temple - and wherein thou art are many things recorded - which I do speak of. Ye shall see these recordings when thou doth enter into the secret place of Mine abode. I say ye shall read the records wherein are written the records of all thy travels from the time ye left the Father Mother God until thine return unto him.

WHAT IS MICHAEL'S FLAMING SWORD? - "The "Sword of Truth and justice."

Recorded by Sister Thedra

Other Books by TNT Publishing

Who am I and Why Am I here?

The Significance of Existence

Death and the Incredible Life After

Fear of Death Removed

Paradise Regained

Spiritual Laws Revealed

Unseen Forces

Too Good to Be True

The Truth of Life in the Spirit World

He Who Has Ears

The Great Awakening, Volumes I thru VII

The Great Awakening, Volume VIII,
THE WHITE STAR OF THE EAST

The Great Awakening, Volume IX,
I THE LORD GOD SAY UNTO THEM

The Great Awakening, Volume X,
MINE INTERCOM MESSAGES FROM THE REALMS OF LIGHT

The Great Awakening, Volume XI,
THE BOOK OF THE LORD

The Great Awakening, Volume XII thru XV,
TEMPLE TEACHINGS FROM THE HIGHER REALMS

Transfiguration Volumes I thru Volume VIII

Contact us at

Email: goldtown11@gmail.com

Web: https://www.whoamiandwhyamihere.com/

www.ingramcontent.com/pod-product-compliance
Lightning Source LLC
LaVergne TN
LVHW051546070426
835507LV00021B/2441